Effective Consultancies in Development and Humanitarian Programmes

Oxfam GB

Oxfam GB, founded in 1942, is a development, humanitarian, and campaigning agency dedicated to finding lasting solutions to poverty and suffering around the world. Oxfam believes that every human being is entitled to a life of dignity and opportunity, and it works with others worldwide to make this become a reality.

From its base in Oxford in the United Kingdom, Oxfam GB publishes and distributes a wide range of books and other resource materials for development and relief workers, researchers and campaigners, schools and colleges, and the general public, as part of its programme of advocacy, education, and communications.

Oxfam GB is a member of Oxfam International, a confederation of 12 agencies of diverse cultures and languages which share a commitment to working for an end to injustice and poverty – both in long-term development work and at times of crisis.

For further information about Oxfam's publishing, and online ordering, visit www.oxfam.org.uk/publications

For information about Oxfam's development, advocacy, and humanitarian relief work around the world, visit www.oxfam.org.uk

Effective Consultancies in Development and Humanitarian Programmes

John Rowley and Frances Rubin

Oxfam

Front cover (left to right)
Taredji Market, St. Louis region, Senegal: Banel Ly of Union des Jeunes Agriculteurs du
    Koyli-Wirndé (UJAK) talking to market traders (Ami Vitale/Oxfam)
Azzazneh, Occupied Palestinian Territories: remedial education classes
    (Jonathan Rainsford/Oxfam)
Santo Domingo, Peru: first ever meeting of all the women's groups in the Piura region
    (Annie Bungeroth/Oxfam)
Spine
Kampong Speu, Cambodia: a provincial Land Dispute Settlement Commission hearing
    (Howard Davies/Oxfam)
Back cover
Allahabad, India: a consultant working with the urban programme in North India mobilises
    a community which is demanding ration cards as a basic right (Jitendra Kumar Maurya)

First published by Oxfam GB in 2006

© Oxfam GB 2006

ISBN 978 0 85598 500 4

ISBN 0 85598 500 3

A catalogue record for this publication is available from the British Library.

Available from:
Bournemouth English Book Centre, PO Box 1496, Parkstone, Dorset, BH12 3YD, UK
tel: +44 (0)1202 712933; fax: +44 (0)1202 712930; e-mail: oxfam@bebc.co.uk

USA: Stylus Publishing LLC, PO Box 605, Herndon, VA 20172-0605, USA
tel: +1 (0)703 661 1581; fax: +1 (0)703 661 1547; e-mail: styluspub@aol.com

For details of local agents and representatives in other countries, consult our website:
www.oxfam.org.uk/publications
or contact Oxfam Publishing, Oxfam House, John Smith Drive, Cowley, Oxford,
OX4 2JY, UK.
tel: +44 (0)1865 473727; e-mail: publish@oxfam.org.uk

Our website contains a fully searchable database of all our titles, and facilities for secure
online ordering.

Published by Oxfam GB, Oxfam House, John Smith Drive, Cowley, Oxford, OX4 2JY, UK.

Printed by Information Press, Eynsham

Oxfam GB is a registered charity, no. 202 918, and is a member of Oxfam International.

Contents

List of figures

List of tables

List of boxes

Acknowledgements

Both authors are especially grateful to Deborah Eade and Nicky May for reading and advising on early drafts of this book, and to Margaret Newens for her comments on the final draft. John Rowley thanks Kate Lonsdale for insight into a particular problem and David Wilson for help with chapter 10; the Vicky Arms Group and the Soup Group for general advice and encouragement; Peggy and Joe Todd for making Guard's Cottage available; and Julia Tait for her support and patience. Frances Rubin is grateful for the support of Corinne Richards, Rosemary Galli, Hugo Jackson, Dr V. Bliznyuk, Jacqui Squire, and Pookie Rubin.

In the process of writing this guide we have spoken to a wide range of consultants and staff in international NGOs and other organisations working in the field of development, both in the UK and around the world. In particular we thank the following people who shared their experience and insights with us by completing an e-mailed questionnaire or taking part in interviews.

Jerry Adams (INTRAC), Catherine Allen (Concern), Aimee Ansari (Oxfam GB), Paul Anticoni (BRCS), Fareed Arthur, Nicholas Atampugre, Julian Barr (ITAD), Maggie Baxter (Womankind), Jon Bennett, Vicky Blagborough (WaterAid), Elizabeth Wade Brown (CAFOD), Margie Buchanan-Smith, Andrew Couldridge, Chris Dammers, Ros David (ActionAid), Michelle Dennison (Oxfam GB), Matt Desmond, Bridget Dillon (DFID), Ed Downs, Deborah Eade (Oxfam GB), Jean Ellis (CES), Sue Enfield, Kate Gant, Joe Gomme, Liz Goold, Brendan Gormley (DEC), Richard Graham (Comic Relief), Alistair Hallam (Valid), Mohammed Hamza, Teresa Hanley (BRCS), Maurice Herson (Oxfam International), Dave Hockaday (Oxfam GB), Kate Horne, Mike Wilson Jarvis (Oxfam GB), Ancilla Kazirukanyo (ActionAid), Annie Lloyd, Maitrisara, Carmen Malena, Linda Mason (Oxfam GB), Isobel McConnan, Alexander Menezes,

(Christian Aid), John Mitchell (ALNAP), Robert Moss, Colin Nee (CES), Koos Neefjes, Margaret Newens (Oxfam GB), Nellie Nyang'Wa (Oxfam GB), David Ould (Anti-Slavery International), D. Parkes (WWF), Derek Poate (ITAD), Johnathan Potter (People in Aid), Michael Powell, Tahmina Rahman, Sarah Reber (BRCS), Malcolm Ridout (Africa Now), Omar da Rocha (Oxfam GB), Nick Roseveare (Oxfam GB), Joss Saunders (Oxfam GB), Richard Sexton, Jill Shankleman, Julie Shrestha (ActionAid), David Smith (Aids Alliance/SCF), Howard Exton Smith, Jeremy Spafford, Jane Stanton (ITAD), Francis Sullivan (WWF), Aidan Timlin (Christian Aid), Karen Twining, Brian Wall (IFRC), Tina Wallace, Sue Weaver, Jill White, Peter Wiles, Colin Williams, Glen Williams, Peter Williams, Suzanne Williams, and Valli Yanni.

(The institutional affiliations in this list may have changed since our survey took place.)

John Rowley and Frances Rubin
August 2006

Some definitions

In this book, the term *consultancy* refers to a defined time-bound assignment, designed to be carried out by a consultant. The word *consultancy* can also be used to mean a company or organisation that gives expert advice in a particular field.

The parties (stakeholders) involved in consultancies

Client: we use the word *client* to mean the person or organisation for whom the consultancy work is being done.

Consultant: a consultant is someone who is carrying out a defined piece of work for a client. In most cases the consultant is external to the organisation that commissions the work.

Commissioner: it is common to use the word *commissioner* for the person in an organisation who hires a consultant to carry out a particular assignment. The commissioner is usually the manager of the consultancy, but he or she could authorise the necessary input and assign the management to someone else.

Consultancy manager: we use the word *manager* in some places to describe the person, usually a client staff member, who is organising the consultancy.

Contractor: we use this word to mean a person or organisation who undertakes a contract to provide goods or services. It is often used to denote commercial consultancy companies that sub-contract individual consultants to carry out work for clients.

Freelance consultant: a person who works for a range of different clients as a solo independent consultant.

Stakeholders: individuals or organisations, either internal or external to the client organisation, who have an interest in a particular piece of work.

Documents relating to consultancies

Call for Tenders: an invitation from a client to consultants to produce a tender for a piece of work. The Call for Tenders describes the task and asks consultants to explain how they would do the work and why they are particularly well qualified to do it.

Contract: the legal document that sets out the terms and conditions of the engagement of a consultant.

Expression of Interest (EoI): a document from a consultant or consultancy group that explains very briefly why they are interested in a particular piece of work and capable of doing it. The client will ask some of those who submit an EoI to develop a full tender.

Tender: a formal proposal from a consultant or consultancy group to carry out a piece of work.

Terms of Reference (ToR): a document that describes the work required of a consultancy.

International development

We use the phrase *international development* to cover two types of programme: humanitarian work done in emergencies, and long-term development work. Principally we focus on the programmes of non-government organisations, but we take account of multilateral and bilateral agencies too.

Bilateral agency: a government department that manages its country's international co-operation activities, including aid funding.

International non-government organisation (INGO): a large international agency, usually with charitable or non-profit status.

Multilateral agency: an international organisation, such as the European Union, the World Bank, or a United Nations body: UNHCR, UNDP, UNICEF, FAO, for example.

1 | Introduction

Organisations working in international development use consultants to carry out a wide variety of tasks. Indeed the reported growth in their use seems to have occurred both in large government agencies and in non-government organisations (NGOs), both national and international. It is said to be due partly to attempts to reduce core staff costs, and partly to those organisations' need for greater flexibility. Whatever the cause, it is important to make the best use of consultancies. This book suggests ways of improving the inputs of all concerned parties, so that both the outcomes and the processes of consultancies are more effective and useful.

Who is this book for?

In this book we examine aspects of consultancy common to all fields as well as the specific nature of consultancy work in international development, with a focus on international NGOs (INGOs) and their national and international partners. The book has been written with the following key audiences in mind:

- staff of NGOs and other types of international humanitarian and development organisation who are responsible for selecting and using consultants;
- people who have to work with consultants who have been selected by others;
- people working in the wider non-profit sector, for example in statutory and voluntary organisations, membership organisations, and community groups;
- people who provide consultancy services to these and other similar organisations;
- people who are thinking of becoming consultants.

The book is intended as a guide to basic good practice in the selection and use of consultants, helping both those who use consultants (*clients*) and those who provide services (*consultants*). We will explain the stages of a typical consultancy, step by step, paying particular attention to the practical, ethical, and legal aspects, but also addressing the importance of the human relationships involved in consultancy work. We believe that consultants could be more competent in serving the needs of clients, and clients could improve the way in which they work with consultants, with only relatively minor changes in the way that consultancies are organised and conducted.

Why was it written?

Many managers successfully hire consultants, and the consultants carry out good work. Some larger organisations, at least in the UK, have begun to develop policies and guidance for staff on the hiring of consultants. This may be part of a general move to 'professionalise' the NGO sector and to improve management systems. Nevertheless, our own experience of hiring and managing consultants, and working as freelance consultants ourselves, has shown us many opportunities to improve standards through the sharing of good practice and the promotion of mutual understanding between clients and consultants.

People working in international development frequently ask us questions such as the following:

Clients

Where can we find someone to work with us on ...?

How much should we pay a consultant?

What do I need to put in the Terms of Reference?

What expenses should we pay for?

How much time should we allow for this piece of work?

Consultants

What fee should I be prepared to accept?

Why do clients always call me at the last minute?

How is it that different departments of the same organisation treat consultants in such different ways?

It is not easy to find publications that give direct answers to such questions. Very few books relate specifically to consultancies in the international development sector; most of the available publications relate to the commercial sector, and they deal with management consultancy.

Also most of the available texts deal with only one side of the work: they aim either to help consultants to be better consultants, or to help clients to get the best out of consultants. This guide focuses on the specific nature of consulting for international non-government development organisations and aims to help clients and consultants respectively to understand each other's roles and responsibilities. Furthermore, we give some consideration to stakeholders who have to receive consultancies organised by others.

Besides reflecting on our own experience, and the insights and experience of a wide range of practitioners, we have drawn on several key resources, listed in the annotated bibliography at the back of this book. We have made particular use of information about contracts, fees, and expenses contained in a document prepared by Sterling Management Consultants for the training of Oxfam GB staff.[1]

The book examines three key areas that affect all consultancies: **context**, **relationships**, and **management**. We will briefly explain some aspects of these three dimensions as they affect consultancy work in the field of international development. These issues will be explored and addressed more fully throughout the book.

The context of consultancies in international development

Consultancy work in the international development sector is similar to consultancy work in other sectors, in that it normally involves people from outside an organisation working on a distinct piece of work for a defined period of time. However, international development work has many specific features of its own: they include working across great geographical distances, often in situations of instability and rapid change, for a large number of different interested parties.

International NGOs are similar to many other types of international organisation, in that their headquarters, regional offices, and national offices may be located in different countries. This fact requires staff and consultants to work across a wide range of cultures and languages; it also means that some of the management of a consultancy is likely to be conducted from a distance.

The nature of international development means that programme work often takes place in unstable, even dangerous, situations. There are physical risks, but also risks of disruption and frequent changes of plan. In certain situations the work may be very urgent, because lives and livelihoods are at risk.

A major feature of the dynamics of international development is that a wide range of stakeholders and organisations are involved, and they may each have different expectations of any particular consultancy. It is common, for example, for work to be carried out by one agency and funded by another, each needing different outcomes from the consultancy that has been commissioned. The differing timetables of different organisations may mean that one agency requires a consultancy to take place at a time that is inconvenient or inappropriate for another stakeholder.

The aid environment has been changing: donors are now demanding professionalism, transparency, and accountability of both government and non-government actors. The use of resources and the overall impacts of activities are being scrutinised more closely, particularly to assess whether they contribute to reductions in poverty. There is an increasing emphasis on organisational development and capacity building, and this changes what is expected of a consultancy.

Many organisations declare a desire to learn more from their work. Consultancies can and should be a major tool for learning. However, the way in which consultancies are structured often prevents learning: short, time-pressured assignments permit very little interaction among consultants and staff and other key stakeholders; the result is that important lessons are lost when the consultants finish their work, leaving the organisation to move on to deal with new priorities. Consultancies cannot systematically assist learning within an organisation unless there is a supportive policy in place and resources, namely staff time, systems, and procedures that are focused on supporting learning. Lack of such a policy may lead to repeated bad practice and a failure to learn from experience.

Relationships

The predominance of short-term consultancy assignments means that the people involved must quickly understand each other in order to work together easily. The relationships between the key people are the most important factor in determining the success or failure of a consultancy. Although it is helpful to improve understanding of the steps and stages of the consultancy process, to plan more thoroughly, and to have clear policies and procedures, these measures will not compensate for problems encountered when people do not understand each other easily.

The key relationship between the client and consultant is both commercial and professional. The client buys the professional services that the consultant sells. It is important to recognise that the consultant is trying to make a living, as well as to provide a service. The client is trying to procure services within a budget, but the manager's livelihood is not involved in the relationship. Relationships may be harmed if either party fails to understand the pressures to which the other is subject.

Particular power dynamics influence the effectiveness of consultancies:

- A consultant may be in a particularly powerful position in relation to staff whose jobs may be changed as a result of the consultancy.
- Consultants are likely to be in an unduly powerful position when they meet members of a community that is the focus of the work of a development agency, particularly if they have been chosen and are paid by an organisation that is funding the work that is the subject of the assignment.
- Power dynamics are also affected by differences related to gender and ethnicity within the consultancy team, between consultant and client, and between consultant and other interested parties ('stakeholders').
- There may be tensions between international and local consultants working on the same assignment. The international consultants may have privileged access to key information from the client's head office, and in practical terms they are likely to be earning more than the local consultants, irrespective of their age and experience.

Consultants need to develop good working relationships with the various stakeholders and gain their trust as rapidly as they can. This is especially important (and potentially more difficult) if some of them may be affected negatively by the outcome of the consultancy. Consultants need good social skills and must be alert to the feelings of others.

Management of the process

Most consultancies require some flexibility in their management. This is particularly the case in international development, where the uncertain context, described above, requires nimble and rapid management responses.

Management of consultancies is more difficult if those in charge are uncertain about the steps and stages that they need to go through. The client and consultant may have different perceptions of how the assignment should be organised, but making their views explicit can improve mutual understanding.

Different assignments will require different approaches, and different levels of responsibility can be devolved to the consultant as a result. It is important to understand that there are different models for managing consultancies, and to select an appropriate approach for each different situation. In Chapter 3 we examine a range of consultancy models and explore how to assign responsibility for each element of a consultancy. Management of a consultancy is easier when the assignment of responsibilities is explicit.

There will always be situations which need urgent responses, but routine consultancy work can and should be programmed to allow adequate time to adopt a sound approach that is consistent with the values of the client organisation. Many NGOs have adopted explicit commitments to respect social diversity and to work in a participatory manner within their own operations and in the project work that they support. The structuring of much consultancy work, including rapid engagement of consultants and tight timescales, often demanded by third parties such as donors, is contradictory to the values of many organisations and can make it very difficult for both clients and consultants to fulfil these commitments.

Conclusion

The aims of this guide can be summarised as follows.

- To explain what services consultants can provide, and how and why clients use them.

- To describe the main steps and stages in a typical consultancy process, identify danger points where things can go wrong, and suggest how to overcome problems.

- To examine some simple models of consultancy and to explain the range of approaches to it, and the roles and responsibilities commonly adopted by each party.

- To explore the importance of the key relationships in the consultancy process and the many actors involved.

- To present the different ways of calculating fees and expenses, to provide a more objective basis for discussions and negotiation.

- To describe different types of contract and some of the important legal issues raised by consultancy work.

- To introduce ethical issues and matters of good professional conduct that need to be considered.

- To consider the process from the perspectives of both clients and consultants, to help each side to understand the position of the other and develop more effective working relationships.

2 | Consultants, clients, and stakeholders

This chapter considers who consultants are and what they do. It discusses the reasons why clients hire consultants; and identifies the various stakeholders who are involved in or affected by a typical consultancy in the international development sector.

What is a consultant?

A consultant is someone who is hired to give expert advice to an organisation, who is normally external to that organisation, and who may also contribute to the process of planning how to provide the services required. Milan Kubr[2] has written a comprehensive guide on working effectively with management consultants. He presents four key criteria that distinguish their work.

First, they provide the service that the client requires, drawing on their own knowledge, expertise, or experience. Consultants are able to work in a completely focused way on a specific task. This is something that staff members are rarely able to do, because they usually have to deal with a wide range of competing priorities in their daily work.

Second, consultants have skills in working with clients. They know that each assignment will involve specific issues and particular personalities, and they use social and communication skills in addition to any specialist technical skills that they may bring to the work.

Third, consultants are independent and are concerned to maintain their objectivity and be seen to be genuinely unbiased in their work. They must be able to give the client the best possible objective advice, without considering the consequences for themselves. The client must feel confident that the consultant can be relied on to behave in a totally independent way.

Fourth, Kubr says that consultants have chosen to adopt a strict ethical approach and adhere to a rigorous code of conduct. In some cases this may be an official code, supported by a professional body such as an association for lawyers or engineers; in other cases, individuals and companies may produce their own codes of conduct. In any event, the consultant must always work in the client's best interests. Good consultants develop a relationship of trust with the client, and their commitment to the client is clear.

Individual consultants providing services to organisations in the international development sector may describe themselves according to their particular specialisation or experience, for example as 'international development consultant', 'social development consultant', 'planning and evaluation consultant', 'environmental consultant', 'socio-economist', 'governance expert', 'organisational development consultant', and so on.

There are few formally agreed standards among consultants. In many countries anyone can establish a consultancy service, with no external verification of their credentials. Some occupations have a professional association to regulate members' performance, and membership of the association is virtually essential in order to operate. The professional body provides some guarantee of the performance of its members, and provides its members with some protection. Many commercial consultancies providing services have signed up to international quality standards as a way of giving some assurance to potential clients, in particular the International Standards Organisation (ISO) 9000 series. We have been unable to find any widely recognised certification or accreditation of consultants' work in the NGO and voluntary sector. Consultants are therefore obliged to develop their own code of professional conduct and systems of quality control. Some networks of consultants are developing voluntary codes of conduct, and at least one non-profit consultancy organisation we spoke to adheres to the Code of Conduct for Consultants provided by the British Quality Foundation. This useful framework may be viewed on the Foundation's website: www.quality-foundation.co.uk.

Many freelance consultants have spent some time working within organisations in the international development sector (in INGOs or in multilateral or bilateral donor agencies); they therefore have an understanding of how such organisations work, and they often share a great deal of their values. Such a background is not indispensable, but it is preferable that consultants share the same overall development objectives as their clients, which in this case could be summed up as a commitment to social and economic justice.

In summary: external consultants can provide support to many areas of work. They adhere more or less to the same sets of values as their client organisations – in this case, a commitment to social and economic justice – and they control their own ethical and professional conduct. They are distinct from members of staff, because they do not work within the management structure of their clients' organisations. They provide independent support and advice; they have no direct control over the work that follows their inputs; they remain outside the organisation that they are advising; and they leave when the assignment is completed.

What services do consultants provide?

Essentially, consultants provide skills, knowledge, information, independence, and extra capacity. In some situations a consultant may be providing several of these inputs in a single consultancy.

Skills, knowledge, information, experience

Consultants have important roles to play in providing skills and knowledge that the staff of an organisation may not possess. This may be a matter of technical expertise: for example, knowledge of agricultural systems, or the transmission and prevention of HIV/AIDS. It could be how to develop better monitoring and evaluation procedures, or how to devise a fundraising plan or an advocacy strategy. It may be in-depth knowledge of particular issues or places. It could be training or planning for a specific piece of work. Consultants may facilitate meetings, to enable all the staff to take part and to prevent the discussion being dominated by any particular agenda or member of staff. They may on occasion be called upon as mediators, to resolve conflicts.

Independence

A consultant should be free from an organisation's internal politics and able to provide clear, constructive advice from a detached and objective perspective. The consultancy will lose its value if it is seen as being partial: as biased towards the position of one particular staff member or interest group, for example. Nor should the consultant be pursuing a personal research project or political agenda. See Chapters 7 and 8 for a discussion of recruitment methods which try to minimise these problems.

As consultants gradually do more work for an organisation and become more familiar with its programmes, culture, and style, they may become increasingly useful to a particular manager. At the same time, this familiarity may mean that they are less able to take an independent, detached view. In such circumstances they have a duty to assess their own ability to be independent, and should warn the client if the relationship seems to be getting too close, or might be perceived as being too close. If a consultant is not able to raise issues or offer criticism freely, or give bad news frankly, he or she needs to withdraw from working for that client for a while.

Extra capacity

There is often work that needs to be done, but it cannot be done by core staff who are working full-time on routine matters. They might be perfectly able to do the work; but there may be time constraints. If a clearly defined piece of work can be identified, then using consultants may be the best way to get the work done.

In some cases, a reduction in core funding in favour of project funding may mean that organisations need to reduce core staff costs. As a result, there are fewer staff to do the existing work, and it is tempting to increase the use of consultants. However, if staff have less time to do their ongoing work, they may not be able to spare the time required to provide a good briefing or guidance to a consultant. It is important to set aside enough time to manage a consultancy. Using a consultant may sometimes be a false economy for hard-pressed staff.

Consultants can be useful to members of staff who may not have time for research and exploring new ideas because of the everyday demands of their jobs. In some cases it may not be necessary for staff to spend a great deal of time reading original texts and attending conferences: instead, consultants can do the research and provide a rapid overview, which may be enough to keep staff informed of new thinking, or to help managers to decide whether or not to invest in a particular area of work.

When consultants are employed to manage an office or a project for an organisation, to represent that organisation, and to be responsible for its resources, they are really acting as staff, even if only for a short time – as part of an emergency response, for example. In such situations, although it may seem cheaper and simpler to hire consultants, it may be more appropriate to hire people as temporary staff. Clients may be in breach of labour laws if they recruit a consultant to manage a piece of work when they should in fact recruit a member of staff on a short-term contract. See Chapter 10 on legal matters, use the checklist in Annex 4, and take further advice if necessary.

Why do clients call in consultants?

Milan Kubr suggests five common reasons for calling in a management consultant: curiosity, insecurity, the need for an alibi, a desire to improve performance, and a need for learning.[3] Some of these reasons may apply to the hiring of consultants in international development work.

- **Curiosity:** maybe a manager has heard of a well-known consultant in a particular field and decides to see what he or she may have to offer the organisation. For example, a well-known academic or practitioner may be invited to run a half-day seminar for staff, or work for a couple of days with the senior management team.

- **Insecurity**: a manager may feel insecure for a number of reasons. It could be that the organisation is experiencing high staff turnover, or there is new competition from younger specialist organisations, or a new aid context may require the organisation to adapt its methods or policies. Calling in a consultant may help managers to think through their responses to these challenges.

- **Self-defence**: it is not uncommon for a consultant to be called in so that a manager can refer to an external expert when needing to justify a decision. This is especially the case if the decision is likely to be unpopular. Or a consultant's report can be used as evidence that a matter has been investigated, even if no action is taken. These are somewhat negative reasons for calling in expensive help!

- **Improving performance**: it is probably true that most consultancies in the international development sector are commissioned out of a genuine desire to improve the impact of a project or programme or other piece of work.

- **Learning**: learning has become an important issue for development agencies, and many initiatives are focused on improving learning or helping to develop 'learning organisations'.

To Kubr's five reasons for calling in a consultant, most INGOs in the development sector would want to add a sixth: the need to *demonstrate accountability to stakeholders*: to check how resources have been used, and with what effect. INGOs are accountable to multiple constituencies: the communities whom they aim to support, their partners, their donors (governments, the private sector, and individuals), and the wider public. There is a tendency to prioritise accountability towards donors, but accountability to partners and local communities is equally important.

Commissioning consultancies in order to learn what works, what does not work, and what impact an initiative has made is also a form of being accountable to those who have provided resources. Conducting consultancies to enable people to have a say in work that affects them is another form of accountability.

The stakeholders in a consultancy

In any proposed assignment it is important to consider the various parties who will have an interest in the process and outcomes: the stakeholders. It is useful to do a 'stakeholder analysis' to assess who is going to be affected, and how, and who may support or obstruct the work.

The identities of the stakeholders will vary. A consultancy that is purely internal to the organisation may have relatively few stakeholders, who are all in similar positions. An evaluation of a programme may involve interactions with several teams, communities, and external organisations.

Experienced clients and consultants will take care to identify all the potential stakeholders, to ensure the appropriate levels of involvement. Consultants must be able to analyse the potential impact of interventions on the various groups involved, and how relationships between them may change as a result. It is rare for an organisation working in international development to have a simple, direct relationship with a single group of people with whom it is working. Consultants need to be sensitive to the web of relationships that has been constructed over time. This is particularly important in international development, where they may be working across different cultures and may need to be particularly sensitive to the location of power in the range of relationships that they are dealing with.

Consider, for example, the evaluation of a programme involving an emergency response to a flood. Potentially all of the following are stakeholders:

- the communities living in the affected area;
- the local community organisations that provided assistance;
- a national NGO which provided support to the local organisations;
- an international NGO which arranged funding and some support in terms of personnel, logistics, and needs assessment;
- national and local government agencies responsible for responding to disasters;
- the donors who provided funds to the INGO;
- the consultants who evaluated the emergency work contracted by the INGO.

The various clients in a consultancy

So far we have used the term *client* generically, referring to an organisation for which a consultant works, or the actual manager of the commission. In fact it is usually possible – and important – to identify a number of clients with whom the consultant must interact in the course of an assignment. Typically four distinct client roles can be identified.

- **The contract client**: the person who will be responsible for drawing up the contract, approving payments, and making some of the administrative arrangements. (In some organisations, this work may be done by a separate contracts department.)

- **The contact client**: the person who deals directly with the consultant. He or she makes the first contact and acts as the first point of contact for all queries, provides the Terms of Reference (ToR), deals with problems, and receives reports.

- **The ultimate client**: the person who must finally be satisfied that the work has been done, even though he or she may not be directly involved. The consultancy might have been commissioned by a donor, or by the organisation's Board or Chief Executive, for example.

- **The user client**: the person who must take action on the results of the consultancy. He or she may be required to implement the recommendations, receive training, change his or her methods of working, or implement a new project.

It may help to consider an example. Suppose that the manager in the head office of an agency authorises a consultancy that will be overseen by a country programme manager located in another country. The country programme manager contracts a consultant to visit a particular project, in order to provide support to the project manager. The project manager will eventually have to implement and use the results of the consultancy work.

In this case, the **ultimate client** is the manager in the headquarters or regional head office. He or she wants proof that the project is doing well and is supporting the programme. The **contract client** may be an administrator in the head office or the regional office, or someone in a dedicated 'contracts department' whose job is to ensure that the consultant is contracted correctly, that the consultancy runs smoothly until it is completed, and that the consultant is paid. The **contact client** is likely to be a manager in the relevant country office: the key person with whom the consultant interacts. He or she wants the project to succeed, but may have to accept that there are weaknesses that need to be addressed. The contact client needs the consultancy to work well and deliver usable results, and also wants the ultimate client to be satisfied with the outcome of the consultancy. The **user client** is the project manager. He or she needs the consultancy to work well; wants to demonstrate good work; seeks congratulations for a job well done; and needs some simple, usable recommendations that can be implemented at the local level.

In small organisations, or a situation in which a single client hires a consultant to work exclusively for him or her, the different roles outlined above will all be fulfilled by the same person.

A responsible consultant will do everything possible to discover the origin of the work and identify all the relevant stakeholders. A responsible client will explain the background to the consultancy and will identify the key interested parties for the benefit of the consultant. In fact, it must be the responsibility of both sides to clarify these matters from the beginning of the consultancy. Such open discussions cannot be achieved unless a certain level of trust has been built up, and that is the first task of both sides when negotiating an assignment. Clients want to be sure that those whom they hire will be able to interact successfully with the network of stakeholders. These are the *psycho-sociological and communication skills* that Kubr considers to be essential qualities of a good consultant.

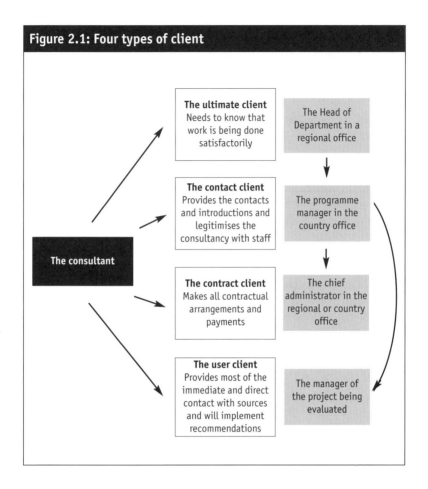

Figure 2.1: Four types of client

The consultant

The ultimate client
Needs to know that work is being done satisfactorily

The Head of Department in a regional office

The contact client
Provides the contacts and introductions and legitimises the consultancy with staff

The programme manager in the country office

The contract client
Makes all contractual arrangements and payments

The chief administrator in the regional or country office

The user client
Provides most of the immediate and direct contact with sources and will implement recommendations

The manager of the project being evaluated

Figure 2.1 illustrates how a consultant has to relate to a range of different people with different perspectives and different needs, and then judge how to develop the consultancy so that it meets the most important of those needs.

Where do consultancies take place?

Given the nature of development and humanitarian work, a consultant or team of consultants may be required to spend considerable time away from home, often in difficult circumstances. In particular, consultants who are required to carry out field work as part of their assignment need to be ready to deal with unpredictable schedules and last-minute changes made necessary by the security situation or other unforeseen circumstances.

'You've got to have flexibility on both sides in our context. I had four people lined up to go to (…), and then the border was closed one day before their briefing, so we decided to try again later.'
(A manager)

There are also more straightforward assignments, such as desk studies and office-based facilitation and training, which will not require complex travel arrangements.

3 | Approaches to consultancy

This chapter presents models of different approaches to consultancy work. We consider the types of task that are involved in consultancies, and then we examine how responsibilities for them can be assigned in different ways.

There is no single correct format for a consultancy: the purpose of the work should define the way in which it is done. In discussing some models, we address two main issues to be considered when designing a consultancy: first, how much of it should be fixed from the start, and how much should be left flexible; and, second, how responsibility for the different steps in a consultancy should be shared between the consultant and the client, and indeed other stakeholders.

The client should consider the precise reasons why a consultant is being sought, and what role the consultant is expected to play. The Association of Consultants and Trainers[4] suggests that answering the following questions will help to define the kind of consultancy required.

- Do you want the consultant to do a specific task, for example draw up a business plan, introduce new technology, devise personnel procedures, or help to restructure a department or the whole organisation? This may be called a *task-based consultancy*.

- Do you want *training*, whereby the consultant helps people to learn specific skills, or increases their awareness of particular issues?

- Do you want the consultant to help people in the organisation to think and talk through what needs to be done about a particular task, and then leave it to the organisation, rather than the consultant, to complete the task? This may be called a *process consultancy* or *facilitation*.

These different types of consultancy require different degrees of preparation and planning. Assignments that are task-based or deliver training may be defined and planned quite tightly, while process work and facilitation require a greater degree of flexibility, to allow the work to be designed as it progresses, in response to interim findings.

Another approach to assessing the kind of consultancy that may be required comes from the work of Edgar Schein, who describes three models.[5] The models form a spectrum of consultancy design, with at one extreme the *expert* who does everything, and at the other extreme the *process supporter* who works alongside the client team.

Model 1: the expert

Consultancy is commonly perceived in terms of hiring 'experts', but this is in fact an extreme form of consultancy. In the 'expert consultancy' model, the consultant works with relatively little involvement of the staff of the client agency, delivering a product or a result that the staff can then incorporate into their work. Think of a mechanic who repairs a car: the client only knows that the car is not working and wants it to work; the mechanic does what is necessary and gives the keys back to the owner, saying that the car now works.

Examples of this kind of consultancy would be the work of computer programmers, finance auditors, and designers of administrative systems. Or it might be a discrete piece of research requested of a consultant because of his or her specific knowledge of a particular geographic area or thematic issue.

The Terms of Reference for this kind of work tend to be tightly defined. Since the client is not involved in the implementation of the consultancy, the effectiveness of the work must be judged by the results. The client will accept the consultancy, provided that the results are delivered. The delivery of the results is effectively the end of the consultancy, and it is possible that a similar piece of work will be required in a number of different offices/work units and at different times. To return to the image of the mechanic and the car that doesn't work: the next time the car breaks down, it will be necessary to call the mechanic again.

One difficulty with this kind of consultancy is that so much depends on the consultant's ability to do a good job. The client may not be able to judge the consultant's competence until presented with the final results of the assignment.

Model 2: the doctor and the patient

In this model of consultancy, the client (patient) knows that something is wrong or needs attention, but is not entirely sure what is required. The client believes that the consultant (doctor) has the skill to complete the diagnosis and propose some action that will improve the situation.

The ToR set out the areas of work to be covered and the types of recommendations to be made, but do not prescribe the final results. By implication the client is not obliged to follow the recommendations, just as a patient is not obliged to take the medicine prescribed by a doctor. Staff in international development agencies are likely to have made assumptions about the nature of the difficulties that they face, and they may need help to see things from a different point of view if the consultant finds a different explanation.

The staff of the agency may be involved in the collection of information and sharing of ideas, but the consultant may well work alone to analyse the data and develop ideas for the future. It is important for the consultant to provide very clear feedback, so that the client can see how the diagnosis was made, and why particular recommendations are made. The entire consultancy can fail if the client cannot see how the consultant reached his or her conclusions.

Model 3: process supporter

In both the models described above, the client sets the consultant a task/problem to take away and solve. In a true process-supporter model, the client retains ownership of the problem, and the consultant helps the client to work through it. The consultant in a process-supporter consultancy works alongside a team of staff, or an individual staff member, to develop a diagnosis of the problem and an appropriate solution. The consultant may also help the staff to define what action to take and how to take it.

In this case, the client may not know what is wrong – in fact, may not even know that something is wrong. What the client needs is support to analyse the situation and develop possible ways forward. The ToR may be fairly open, doing no more than identifying the people with whom the consultant should work, and setting an overall timetable for the work.

It is important not to confuse flexible management of the process with the lack of a clear brief, or the absence of a clear focus on outcomes. It may be said that the details can be worked out as the work progresses, but this approach will not work unless the client and consultant have clear and shared ideas on how the details will be worked out, and what the consultancy is supposed to achieve.

A number of organisations actively support long-term process inputs. For example, one UK-based NGO pays for a number of national consultants in Brazil to work on a call-down basis to accompany the NGO's partner organisations. In another case, an agency has provided on-going consultancy over time to a number of its partners, to help them with monitoring and evaluation. Long-term input may ultimately be no more costly, and may even be cheaper and less disruptive, than one-off short-term consultancies.

Table 3.1: Key differences between two models of consultancy		
	'Expert' model	'Process-supporter' model
Terms of Reference	Very tight	Loose
Involvement of staff	Slight	Continuous
Definition of need	Consultant	Client
Choice of methods	Consultant	Client with consultant
Solution definition	Consultant	Mostly client
Assessment evaluation	Based almost entirely on the results	Based on self-assessment

The need for flexibility

It may be difficult for clients who have relatively little experience of hiring consultants to allow them a great deal of flexibility. There is often a temptation to try to determine and control the consultancy inputs, in order to feel confident that the consultant will deliver what is required – but in fact negotiated responsibilities may be more appropriate. It requires some confidence to launch a consultancy without a very clear overview of how it will proceed, and this confidence normally comes from experience.

The point of presenting the three models described above is to demonstrate that different consultancies may require different behaviours on the part of client and consultant; and any particular consultancy may involve different models at different stages of the process.

Process support and participation

The international development sector has adopted an ideology of participation, and it is widely expected that all stakeholders will participate in some way in initiatives that affect them. This tends to mean that process support is part of all consultancies. It is hard to imagine a consultancy in this sector that could be entirely modelled as an 'expert consultancy'.

Questions of power and control are key concerns for consultants and clients, and they may significantly affect the outcome of a piece of work. A consultancy is more likely to provide constructive help to the client if roles are effectively negotiated, and if the relationship with the consultant is co-operative, rather than trying to enforce a narrow Terms of Reference.

The first discussions of the ToR are a moment when the flexibility or rigidity of the client's approach becomes clear. In our research with consultants, several reported unwillingness on the part of their clients to adjust the ToR. Clients who do not want to negotiate the ToR must be completely confident that they have accurately identified the issues that need to be addressed, and the measures that need to be taken.

Experienced consultants will expect to ask questions about the ToR. They will want to understand how the ToR were developed, and who was involved in the drafting. They will want to understand as early as possible how flexible the client expects to be in the interpretation of the ToR as the work progresses to completion. Clients should be open to suggestions from experienced consultants.

More flexible processes, greater dialogue, and greater co-operation between consultants and clients in the design of consultancy work would almost always be a positive development. Consultants have told us of many situations where the precise nature of the work required cannot be known until the work has started, so some flexibility in defining the work would improve the overall quality of the consultancy. Successful consultancies are based on a clear brief, on clear mechanisms for changing the brief, and on good working relationships that start during the first contacts and are developed through the rest of the consultancy, however short the assignment may be.

This chapter ends with two lists. The first presents the attributes of a good consultant from the perspective of clients, and the second presents the attributes that consultants appreciate in clients.

The attributes of a good consultant

Apart from the specific knowledge and experience required for a particular piece of work, clients who took part in our survey said that they value the following attributes in consultants:

- ability to listen and observe
- good writing and analytical skills
- ability to see things from different perspectives
- ability to employ a variety of research tools and techniques
- ability to deal with different cultural contexts and relationships
- adaptation to the specific context of each piece of work
- flexibility, given that schedules and situations may change, even with the best planning
- honesty about what is not feasible, and what they cannot deliver

- persistence in questioning the consultancy brief or ToR, in order to ensure a shared understanding of the task
- timely reporting
- a willingness to check and discuss any required changes
- empathy with the client organisation.

The attributes of a good client

Consultants whom we interviewed said that they value the following attributes in clients:

- clarity about the issues to be addressed, and the nature of the final product
- clarity about the identities of the stakeholders
- clear policies and guidelines on the contracting of consultants (fees, expenses, etc.)
- efficient contracting and payment procedures
- timely provision of logistical support
- availability for consultation when agreed
- ability to be flexible as situations change
- commitment to learning from the process
- ability to distinguish between bad consultancy practice and bad news
- willingness to provide feedback to consultants
- a human kindness that is welcoming and supportive.

4 | Stages of consultancy

This chapter introduces the stages of consultancy, in a structured form which will be used throughout the book. Figure 4.1 illustrates the key stages of a typical consultancy, in order to provide an overview of the sequence of events.

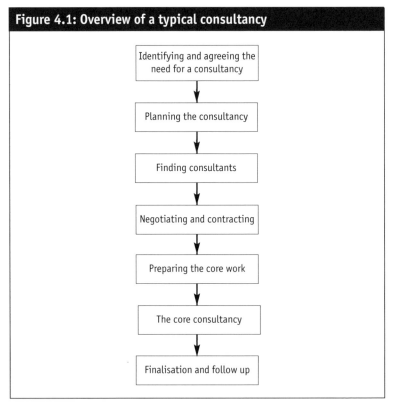

Figure 4.1: Overview of a typical consultancy

Identifying and agreeing the need for a consultancy

↓

Planning the consultancy

↓

Finding consultants

↓

Negotiating and contracting

↓

Preparing the core work

↓

The core consultancy

↓

Finalisation and follow up

These stages are presented from the perspective of the client who is seeking consultancy support. Managing a consultancy means considering the whole sequence of inputs, from identification of the need to finalisation of the assignment and follow-up measures. The more time that is spent in thinking through all the stages and planning ahead, the more smoothly the consultancy is likely to proceed.

While a consultancy can be seen as a straightforward sequence of events, it should also be understood as a set of relationships. How the relationships are initiated and developed by the key stakeholders will fundamentally affect the outcome of the exercise. Although we present the stages as a single straight line, we are aware that the process may include a number of loops, as client and consultants and the wider group of stakeholders negotiate and re-negotiate and manage the work of a consultancy.

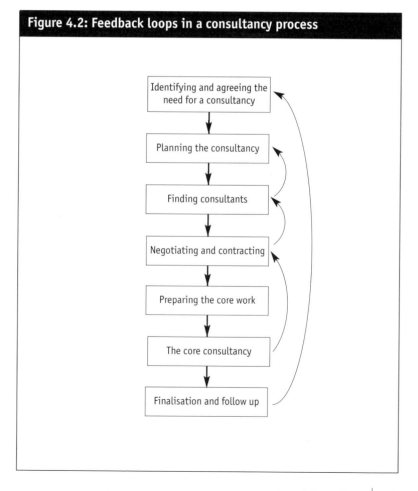

Figure 4.2: Feedback loops in a consultancy process

Identifying and agreeing the need for a consultancy

Planning the consultancy

Finding consultants

Negotiating and contracting

Preparing the core work

The core consultancy

Finalisation and follow up

In Figure 4.2, the largest loop suggests that the end of one consultancy could lead to the start of another. In the smaller loops we can see how the selection of a consultant can lead back to the re-design and planning of the consultancy. Similarly, where a negotiation with one consultant or group fails, the client may need to loop back to finding other consultants.

Perhaps the most important loop in the diagram comes from the core work, requiring a re-negotiation of the contract or the Terms of Reference. This is a common loop, because it is often the case that the work involved in a consultancy does not become clear until the assignment has begun – and a re-negotiation becomes necessary.

Figure 4.3 shows a number of steps within each stage and gives an overview of the issues that will be discussed in the following chapters of the book. The figure covers most of the eventualities of a complex and relatively large consultancy. Many consultancies will be simpler and may by-pass some of the smaller steps. Nevertheless it may be useful to set out as many steps as can be defined, in order to clarify what the process should entail.

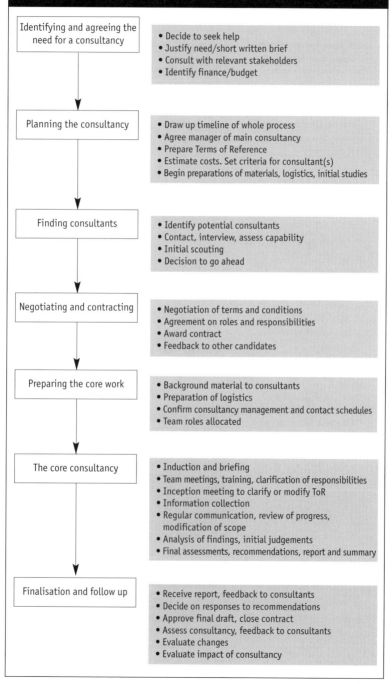

Figure 4.3: Detailed steps and stages in a consultancy

Identifying and agreeing the need for a consultancy	• Decide to seek help • Justify need/short written brief • Consult with relevant stakeholders • Identify finance/budget
Planning the consultancy	• Draw up timeline of whole process • Agree manager of main consultancy • Prepare Terms of Reference • Estimate costs. Set criteria for consultant(s) • Begin preparations of materials, logistics, initial studies
Finding consultants	• Identify potential consultants • Contact, interview, assess capability • Initial scouting • Decision to go ahead
Negotiating and contracting	• Negotiation of terms and conditions • Agreement on roles and responsibilities • Award contract • Feedback to other candidates
Preparing the core work	• Background material to consultants • Preparation of logistics • Confirm consultancy management and contact schedules • Team roles allocated
The core consultancy	• Induction and briefing • Team meetings, training, clarification of responsibilities • Inception meeting to clarify or modify ToR • Information collection • Regular communication, review of progress, modification of scope • Analysis of findings, initial judgements • Final assessments, recommendations, report and summary
Finalisation and follow up	• Receive report, feedback to consultants • Decide on responses to recommendations • Approve final draft, close contract • Assess consultancy, feedback to consultants • Evaluate changes • Evaluate impact of consultancy

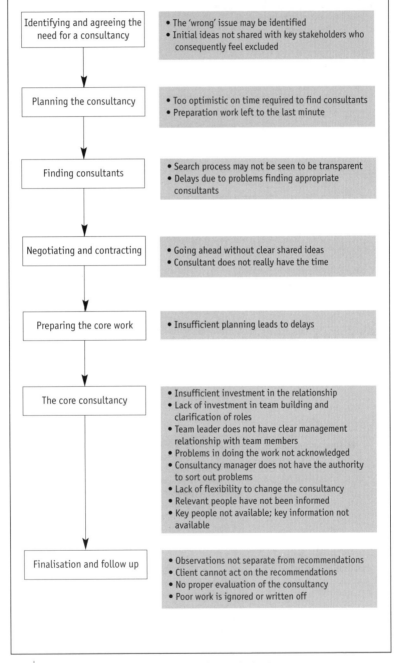

Figure 4.4: Common problems in consultancies

| Identifying and agreeing the need for a consultancy | • The 'wrong' issue may be identified
• Initial ideas not shared with key stakeholders who consequently feel excluded |

| Planning the consultancy | • Too optimistic on time required to find consultants
• Preparation work left to the last minute |

| Finding consultants | • Search process may not be seen to be transparent
• Delays due to problems finding appropriate consultants |

| Negotiating and contracting | • Going ahead without clear shared ideas
• Consultant does not really have the time |

| Preparing the core work | • Insufficient planning leads to delays |

| The core consultancy | • Insufficient investment in the relationship
• Lack of investment in team building and clarification of roles
• Team leader does not have clear management relationship with team members
• Problems in doing the work not acknowledged
• Consultancy manager does not have the authority to sort out problems
• Lack of flexibility to change the consultancy
• Relevant people have not been informed
• Key people not available; key information not available |

| Finalisation and follow up | • Observations not separate from recommendations
• Client cannot act on the recommendations
• No proper evaluation of the consultancy
• Poor work is ignored or written off |

Common problems

Figure 4.4 goes back to the main stages in a consultancy and identifies the typical problems that can occur. The most difficult challenges include the first mentioned: the identification of the 'wrong' problem. Almost everyone whom we interviewed gave examples of this kind of difficulty. The consultant may be asked to work on something that is not the real or core problem. The client may be asked by a donor or a head office to carry out a consultancy that is not desired or required.

The lack of flexibility required to adjust the work of a consultancy was another key problem frequently mentioned to us. Both clients and consultants complained of a rigid attachment to the ToR, despite obvious signals that changes are necessary.

Consultants complained that clients often do not assess the quality or usefulness of consultancy inputs, and fail to give feedback after the work has been completed. In many cases the reason may be the pressure under which clients and consultants work, which pushes them on to think about the next task before there is time to assess the previous one. However, there may be greater problems if the organisation that is contracting the consultant does not sufficiently prioritise learning from the consultancy.

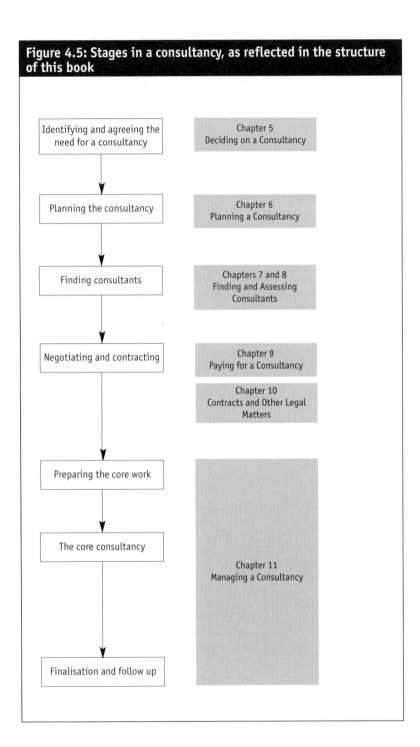

Figure 4.5: Stages in a consultancy, as reflected in the structure of this book

Identifying and agreeing the need for a consultancy	Chapter 5 Deciding on a Consultancy
Planning the consultancy	Chapter 6 Planning a Consultancy
Finding consultants	Chapters 7 and 8 Finding and Assessing Consultants
Negotiating and contracting	Chapter 9 Paying for a Consultancy / Chapter 10 Contracts and Other Legal Matters
Preparing the core work	Chapter 11 Managing a Consultancy
The core consultancy	
Finalisation and follow up	

The chapters that follow deal in some detail with each of the stages and steps, and the common problems that should be avoided. The chapters do not match exactly the stages of the flow diagram in Figure 4.5. Some stages raise more issues and require more than one chapter; other stages can be treated in a single chapter. Later chapters consider a number of issues that do not relate directly to specific stages in the consultancy process: Chapter 12 considers ethical issues that affect all stages, while Chapter 13 examines what it is like to work as a self-employed consultant. Chapter 14 contains checklists of questions for the different stages, to help both clients and consultants to think through a consultancy assignment.

5 | Deciding on a consultancy

This chapter will take readers through the initial stage of identifying the need for a consultancy, justifying that need, and then deciding to proceed.

In some cases the need for a consultancy is very clear, and it may be possible to go very quickly through this stage to more detailed planning, including the key step of drafting the Terms of Reference. Chapter 6 deals directly with drawing up the ToR. In other situations the rationale for a consultancy may not be so evident. In such cases it is useful to develop a justification. This is particularly helpful where it is necessary to gain support for the consultancy from major interested stakeholders before going ahead – especially if the work is not a routine consultancy, and many parts of the organisation are involved. A well-presented justification could make it easier to obtain financial support, either within the organisation or externally.

This chapter also discusses some situations where it would be inappropriate to call in a consultant.

Good consultancies come from good timing and a clear sense of need on the part of the client. Good consultancies tend to occur when key stakeholders feel properly involved in the process and committed to its outcomes. Particular difficulties can arise when a consultancy is felt to be imposed from the outside, for example when an organisation is obliged to agree to an external evaluation that seems to be determined by the needs of the donor rather than by the requirements of the work.

The need for a consultancy might start as an undefined feeling that some aspect of a project or programme should be better: that something is wrong somewhere. Often the symptoms that present themselves to the client may not be the same as the root cause of the problem. This could be because the issue has not been considered in sufficient depth. It is quite common in such situations for consultants to start work, only to find that they should be addressing a different issue from the one identified in their brief. An experienced consultant will always probe the origins of a consultancy during the first contacts with the client.

At this stage the client should identify the key stakeholders. These may include the staff of partner organisations, members of local organisations who may be the focus of the consultancy, staff employed in various parts of the client organisation, and people who will be responsible for approving the necessary resources. It will be necessary to clarify how these different types of stakeholder need to be involved in the work. They may prove to be helpful allies who might provide comments and additional insights on the basis of the statement of justification; they may need to be closely involved in defining what should be covered and how, including suggesting candidates for the work. It is equally important to consider which stakeholders may potentially obstruct the work.

It is critically important for the consultancy manager to keep key stakeholders informed, particularly if the consultant/s will be visiting them later in the process.

Justification for a consultancy

The initial brief statement of justification will facilitate the development of the more detailed Terms of Reference that should form part of the contract with a consultant. Chapter 14 provides a checklist of this stage of the consultancy.

The development of a justification for the consultancy will also help to clarify the skills and experience needed, and to determine whether the work can best be done by a single person or a team. The questions that need to be addressed when seeking consultants are considered in more detail in Chapter 7. Table 5.1 (overleaf) sets out some things to consider when drafting the justification for a consultancy.

Table 5.1: Drafting the justification for a consultancy

Background to the issue	Briefly explain the work of the relevant part of the organisation. Briefly explain what the issue is, and how it arose. This might be most easily expressed as questions to which you want answers.
Why the issue should be addressed with the help of a consultant	Do you need specific skills, experience, information, time, or independent assessment, or some combination of these? See Chapter 2 for advice on what consultants can provide.
Outcomes	What are the possible results of a successful consultancy? Will it lead to clear answers to the questions drafted earlier, and will the answers lead to clear decisions and actions?
Potential benefits from the work	If these answers and decisions are made effectively, what will be the rewards for the project and the organisation?
Ideal schedule, including any fixed dates	The schedule may be easy to establish if there are clear fixed dates (e.g. presentation of the consultant's report at a specific Board meeting). However, it may take longer than expected to find the right person to act as consultant and to arrange meetings with all the necessary people. Add extra time for start-up and for review of the process. Consider any logistical issues that may affect timing, or external factors such as political events, season, availability of stakeholders, public holidays, etc.
Probable costs	Costs need be only approximate at this stage, but it is helpful to work out a rough figure. The estimate may lead to a change in the decision-making process, if the expenditure requires the authorisation of people who have not been involved so far. Consider also if there are ways of achieving the same results without the same level of expense. Would internal consultants achieve the same (or almost the same) results? See Chapter 9.
Roles of the consultant	It may be too soon to define a detailed person-specification, but it would be helpful at this stage to set out some of the work that the consultant(s) will be expected to do, the advice that they would be expected to give, and therefore the range of skills and experience likely to be needed. Attention should be paid to diversity issues: what difference might the sex or ethnic background of the consultant(s) make to the process?
People who should take part or be involved	Who are the different stakeholders? How should they be involved? Who should be asked to participate in developing the ToR and who should be simply made aware that the work will happen? It is important to engage others

	proactively to ensure that they will contribute effectively when necessary. Consider any constraints that may limit the availability of particular people, and measures to mitigate this. There are gender-related questions to ask here: men and women may have different constraints on their availability.
How the consultancy will be managed	Think about the management of the consultancy. Colleagues, partners, and communities will want plenty of notice, so that they can make time available in their schedules. They will also be encouraged if they can see that the consultancy is likely to be well managed, with a good chance of yielding results that will be useful to them.

What consultancies should not be used for

Although there are few absolute rules about the kind of work that consultants can legitimately be asked to do, we can identify some things that are likely to lead to difficulties, and some things that should definitely be avoided.

Management decisions

Consultants can help managers to make decisions by providing information and analysis. Clients should not avoid taking difficult decisions by hiding behind a consultant. If the consultant is being asked to take decisions about management, this indicates either a serious problem, or the need to contract him or her as a temporary member of staff.

Similarly, clients should not invite consultants to make recommendations on management matters if the manager has already decided what he or she wants to do next. Consultants frequently describe assignments on which they worked very hard to formulate recommendations, only to discover that the client had already decided on the next steps. For example, a client organisation has been considering whether or not to open a programme in a new area; the consultant indicates some specific factors for consideration, but finds that the basic decision to proceed has already been taken, possibly because donor funding is available.

Using up time or evading responsibility

Sometimes a consultancy may appear to be the right thing to do because it will give the impression that something important is being done. Or it may be used to buy time: the threat of a strategic programme review may be postponed or even avoided by a decision to commission a consultancy review of a particular office or project. Or it may be used to protect a manager from making an unpopular decision. First, the consultancy process may delay the need to make or announce the decision. Second, the manager may be able to present the decision as inevitable because it results from the consultant's findings. This is dishonest.

Using up money

A consultancy may be commissioned because a budget line is unused, and the end of the financial year is approaching. In some financial systems, money that is not spent in the year is lost to the programme and cannot be carried forward, so it is perceived to be advantageous to spend the money before the year ends. Good work can be done in such a situation, especially if it is an opportunity to do something that has been impossible at other times. However, just because the funds are available is not a good enough reason in itself.

The wrong time for real results

A major cause for concern for both consultants and clients is the project evaluation that is required by a third party, usually a donor. The evaluation may be requested at what seems to be an inappropriate time for those directly involved in the work. If there is good reason to postpone, then there needs to be dialogue between donors, clients, and local partners. At the same time, all parties need to recognise each other's obligations and constraints.

Recommendations that cannot be implemented

A client has problems if an external consultancy seems likely to be useful but the staff or team in question do not seem ready or strong enough to receive what they might perceive as criticism of their work. It would be a waste of resources if recommendations could not be implemented because of a personal or institutional inability to absorb and use feedback. This situation may be improved if both client and consultant are open and share ideas as the work evolves. If the consultant judges that the team will not be able to respond to the forceful recommendations that might be made to a more robust team, he or she may decide to make more moderate recommendations – but should explain the reason to the client. The responsible consultant makes recommendations that can be acted upon. Some team building or individual coaching may be called for in response to the recommendations.

Finally, having asked themselves some difficult questions, it is important that those justifying the need to hire consultancy support are able to state: *This is a legitimate need and not an excuse to avoid a difficult management situation. We are not attempting to find an easy way out of an awkward situation.*

6 | Planning a consultancy

This chapter describes the development of the Terms of Reference (ToR), which is the key step in planning a consultancy. Once it has been decided to proceed with the consultancy, planning for the whole exercise can begin.

Assigning a manager and developing a timeline

The manager of the consultancy will be responsible for ensuring that ToR are drawn up and finalised. It is best if the same person is able to take forward and manage the whole exercise. He or she may or may not be the person who initiated the work. The manager needs to have sufficient authority to negotiate with key stakeholders within and outside the client organisation.

The first task for the manager is to prepare an ideal timeline for the entire process, including the planning phase, the identification and selection of consultants, through to finalisation of the assignment, evaluation of the work, feedback to the consultants, and follow-up actions. Drawing up a timeline should help to identify major problems that might occur in the schedule: for example, holidays, changes of season, end of staff contracts, unavailability of key stakeholders, and other events both internal and external. (See the checklists in Chapter 14.)

The role of the Terms of Reference (ToR)

In Chapter 5, we described the process of developing a statement of justification, which is essentially a draft ToR. The justification is normally an internal document, seeking organisational approval or support for the consultancy. By contrast, the formal Terms of Reference is a document that can be used externally; it specifies the scope and nature of the work, and states what the consultant will be obliged to deliver.

The ToR will be part of the legal contract between the consultant and the client. The final version of the ToR must therefore specify precisely what is required. Consultants have a fear of being told at the end of a piece of work that they have not respected the ToR. This is the same as being accused of breaking a contract or a personal promise: it can be a very serious allegation.

> 'They (the client) asked me for more work on one section, and when I questioned this they said that they would have to check the ToR to see if I had properly fulfilled them. This was clearly a threat not to pay me and to question my professional integrity. This happened a number of times, and I ended up doing a great deal more work than was in the ToR because of this implied threat!'
> (A consultant)

The Terms of Reference should help the client to identify and negotiate with prospective consultants. They should be sufficiently clear to make it obvious what the client wants to achieve, while at the same time allowing scope for consultants to offer suggestions about how the work might be carried out.

It may be appropriate for the client to provide a simple verbal outline of the work that a consultant is required to do and ask the consultant to draw up a more detailed ToR, explaining how the work will be done. This document will then be discussed and agreed with the client. Generally we recommend that relying on purely verbal ToR should be avoided. (See Chapter 10, which deals in detail with legal matters.) Apart from any concerns about legality, the act of writing usually helps clients to clarify what they want to achieve, and helps consultants to understand what they have to do.

Contents of the Terms of Reference

Terms of Reference may be short documents, consisting of a few bullet points, or they may be very detailed and lengthy texts. It will depend on the nature of the task and the nature of the consultant-selection process. In some cases a statement of a problem may be all that it contains, with the expectation of hiring a consultant who will propose how to diagnose the cause and recommend a solution. A formal selection process, including tendering, will require documents that provide more background information. Further details are given in Chapter 8.

The key points that should be covered by the ToR are listed below:

- Title of the consultancy.
- Background to the consultancy.
- Purpose/objectives: why the exercise is being called for, and what it is expected to achieve.

- Scope of the work (for example, a particular work unit, programme, or sector).
- Expected outcomes and products (reports/ documents/ workshops/ video, for example).
- Profile of consultants: an outline of the skills and experience required (see Chapter 7).
- How the work is to be carried out. This may be the most contentious element of the ToR: how tightly does the client want to prescribe the methods to be followed, and how much can be left to the discretion of the consultant?
- Schedule and logistics (within the scope of the consultancy assignment).
- Reporting requirements (during the assignment and at the end).
- Overall timeframe.

In addition, the ToR should provide information about the organisation that is commissioning the consultancy, and the overall approach that is expected. It is often useful to include aspects of the history and values of the organisation. The ToR may state, for example, that the organisation has a commitment to gender equality in all its work, and/or that it expects the consultant to adopt a participatory approach. Such statements will help the consultant to understand what the client expects. Further information about the background of the organisation, together with relevant policy papers, may be provided as appendices or as Web references.

A definition of the type of report required

Almost all consultancies end with a written report, even if the purpose is simply to document the process that has been undertaken. The report is very often the output and the ultimate tool of consultancy work. A good ToR will give clear guidance on the expected readership and uses of the report, and it may also specify the style, structure, and length. (Some international development agencies insist on the use of a prescribed house style, and there is no doubt that it is useful to the client to have reports with a consistent structure, which will make it easier to summarise learning from a series of reports.) It is standard practice to expect consultants to produce summaries of longer reports. Each organisation will have its own guidelines, but a maximum of 5000 words seems to be a reasonable standard for a summary. It should contain a list of the key findings and ensuing recommendations. It is often helpful to summarise key recommendations in a table, with a note to identify to whom they are being addressed.

The main report should be short and concise, with supporting material supplied in the form of annexes. For example, where different team members have been responsible for particular aspects of work, individual members' reports may be added to the main report as appendices. It is generally the Team Leader's responsibility to draw together the key findings and recommendations.

At the planning stage, the language of the report should be agreed, plus the need for translation, if any. Consider the most appropriate format for presenting findings and recommendations to different sets of stakeholders, and particularly to community-level partners. There may be formats that are more appropriate than a written report.

Circulating the draft Terms of Reference

Once the Terms of Reference have been drafted, they should be circulated to key stakeholders for comment. In some situations, for example when determining the objectives and scope of an evaluation of a humanitarian response that needs to involve many actors, the ToR risk becoming very long and detailed. The schedule must therefore allow time for discussion and negotiation between the actors. In this situation, allowing some flexibility to negotiate the ToR at the early stages of the actual evaluation work may help stakeholders to feel that they have been properly involved in the process. It also means that there is an opportunity to ensure that all parties have the same understanding of the purpose of the work, how it is going to be conducted, and the expected outcomes. [6]

Stakeholders who may need to be consulted on the objectives of an evaluation might include partner-agency staff, government policy makers, local officials, UN agencies, beneficiary representatives, and donors.

It is common for the Terms of Reference to go through several drafts at this stage, particularly if they need to be circulated to several stakeholders. If consultation involves parts of the organisation located in different countries, as well as partner organisations, the process of developing the ToR can be quite lengthy, so this phase needs to be factored into the overall timetable.

Sometimes it is appropriate to hire a consultant to design a larger consultancy, part of which involves the preparation of the Terms of Reference. This is sometimes referred to as a 'scoping exercise'. It could be a very simple piece of work, involving little more than careful drafting, or it could be a large piece of work requiring a great deal of research and detailed work, including field visits, as preparation for a larger study. Such a scoping exercise would require its own Terms of Reference. Scoping studies can help to ensure that subsequent consultancy inputs are more effectively targeted.

Negotiating the Terms of Reference

The degree to which ToR are considered negotiable will depend on the type of consultancy proposed, the number of people involved, and the nature of the relationship between the client and consultant. Some consultancies are determined by strict guidelines dictated by a donor and cannot be changed to any great extent. If there are many parties involved, it becomes difficult to keep everyone informed about the changes. The consultancy manager may set out a timetable for the production of the ToR, asking for comments to be delivered by a particular date, and then producing a final version at a later agreed date.

It is reasonable for the consultant, once appointed, to work through the ToR with the client and ask for further information about the context, the nature of the tasks to be carried out, and the possible outcomes of the consultancy. This process need not result in any rewriting of the ToR, but a stage should be reached at which there is a clear and shared understanding of the work. Clients should expect the consultant to ask questions, and they should be ready to provide answers in order to reach the necessary shared understanding.

In the early stages of a consultancy, it is likely that both sides need to adjust their views about what can be done. Terms of Reference are often ambitious in their scope, and they assume ideal performance and good conditions. It is often the case that the full range of the client's requirements is not achievable in the time available. A responsible consultant has a duty to point this out. Experienced clients and consultants will be more realistic about what can be achieved. The management of expectations is an important aspect of preparing a consultancy. Finding a balance between ambitious aims and realistic expectations requires some skill and experience.

Where a consultant has been involved in the development of the ToR, there will be less need for both sides to negotiate the final form of words in the document. Where a client has produced the ToR and presented them to the consultant, there will be a greater need for discussion.

There are many occasions where the precise nature of the work cannot be known at the outset, so the ToR can serve only as a guide. The actual content of the work is developed in a series of steps, as the contract progresses. This approach requires excellent communication between the client and the consultant.

Who is responsible for what?

In most cases the client determines where the balance of responsibilities will lie for the different stages of the consultancy. It can be very helpful in the early stages for the client and the consultant to state explicitly how they each view the balance of responsibility for each of the tasks. Here is a basic task list:

- defining the initial problem
- setting the Terms of Reference
- choosing the methodology to be used
- collecting information
- analysing the information
- choosing the methods for presenting the findings
- deciding who should receive the findings and recommendations
- structuring the report
- defining recommendations
- informing other stakeholders of the results of the consultancy
- extracting main lessons from the consultancy.

Each of the tasks in the list might be categorised in one of the following ways: (1) consultant has complete control, (2) consultant has more control, (3) responsibilities are evenly shared, (4) client has more control, or (5) client has total control.

The consultant and writer Peter Block presents a longer list of the steps in a consultancy. He suggests [7] that a visual exercise will help a consultant to assess where the balance of responsibilities lies. The same exercise could be helpful to clients when they are proposing a consultancy. In Block's exercise, the consultant will put a mark on a line between '100 per cent consultant control' and '100 per cent client control'. A mark on the middle point (50:50) of the line would suggest that the client and the consultant should share the task equally. This kind of exercise might lead to a shared understanding of how the work can be managed. It might also lead to greater levels of trust, as client and consultant share ideas about how to make the consultancy work.

The sections above assume a simple situation where there is one consultant and one client. However, the procedures described here could equally be used to define who is responsible for what when several stakeholders are working on a joint consultancy. This may be helpful where a participatory study is envisaged.

The need to keep written records

In consultancies that run over several months, it is essential to maintain a written record of the exchanges that define any adjustments. If agreements are made verbally, they should be followed up by confirmation in writing. In many small consultancies in the international development sector, work is successfully completed without written ToR, and the shared understanding is good enough to ensure that both sides are satisfied. However, we recommend using written ToR and confirming agreed changes in writing. If the client does not do this, then the consultant should always write, confirming what he or she has understood. This ensures that there is a written record in case any disagreement arises later.

Costing, preparation of materials, logistics, and preliminary studies

As the Terms of Reference are developed, it becomes possible to cost the exercise more precisely. This is also the time to start checking on available resources and logistical support, and to initiate the process of preparing background materials so that they will be ready when the core work of the consultancy begins. Chapter 9 provides more information on financial matters, and Chapter 14 provides checklists to help with preparation.

As soon as it is appropriate, key staff should be briefed on the proposed consultancy and on their roles in it. If members of staff, and other stakeholders, are not properly briefed in a sensitive way, they may show their frustration by withholding their co-operation. The very presence of consultants in an organisation can disrupt routines and require staff to spend time working directly with them, or servicing their needs for information and administrative support. If staff members regard the consultancy as a disruption or interruption to their normal work, or if other stakeholders can see little likely benefit for their efforts (for example, hosting visits of consultants sent by others), they are unlikely to be supportive and helpful.

7 | Finding consultants

In this chapter we discuss the criteria that will help clients to define the profile of the consultant(s) that they need and to assess the suitability of individual candidates. Then we present sources of information on consultants and explain selection procedures step by step.

Searching for and hiring a consultant is somewhat different from staff recruitment. Unless formal tendering is involved, it is normally a less structured process. In routine staff recruitment, a range of people may be involved in drafting the job description, setting the person specification, determining terms and conditions, short-listing and interviewing candidates, and selecting the best person for the job. These stages are likely to involve formal procedures that are determined by organisational policies and procedures and applicable labour law. Involving a range of people provides checks and balances that make the process more rigorous. When hiring a consultant, unless the client decides to use a formal tendering process, and/or to involve key stakeholders such as the partner agency, much of the work may fall on a single person. This may well be the same person who has to justify the procedure and manage the outcome of the consultancy.

It helps to have clear organisational policies and procedures for hiring consultants, in particular by standardising practices across an organisation. Establishing a list of criteria for selection for a particular assignment will also help to increase transparency and accountability; this need for accountability is an important consideration for organisations working in the development sector.

Clear organisational policies would help to define the selection process that should be followed: for example, whether it is appropriate simply to search via personal networks, or whether a more formal tendering process is called for. NGOs and similar organisations will need to balance the need for transparency and accountability against the time and costs involved in this type of procurement process. A list of criteria to help to identify consultants will at least serve to demonstrate that selection was based on finding the most appropriate candidate for the work. When searching through personal networks and contacts for 'tried and tested' consultants, clients should contact and interview several candidates, if at all possible.

When not conducted as part of a formal, structured tendering process, the initial stage of contacting consultants and opening negotiations is where the important relationship between consultant and client begins to be established. All the clients and consultants who we talked to for this book emphasised the need for empathy and shared values, leading to a good rapport between both parties. (This does not necessarily mean that consultants must always be drawn from the voluntary, not-for-profit sector.)

Lack of time is the biggest enemy of good decisions in selecting consultants.

Defining the type of consultant that is required

The following checklist is designed to help clients to identify the overall profile of the consultant(s) that they require. Generally these questions should be addressed at the time of developing the ToR.

- Internal or external – member of staff or consultant?
- Single consultant or team?
- Freelance consultant or consultancy company?
- National or international expertise?
- Familiarity with your organisation?
- Key qualifications and competencies.
- Other essential skills: languages, writing, interviewing, etc.
- Shared values.

Internal or external?

Consultancy need not always be done by someone completely external to the client organisation. There are situations in which complete independence from the organisation is not the most important criterion. In an internal consultancy, a staff person from within the organisation, even if from a different unit, undertakes the assignment. Some larger organisations with many internationally located offices have a considerable pool of skills and experience on which to draw, and in some cases they have specific units set up to provide consultancy, usually of a technical or managerial nature (Public Health, Planning and Learning, Human Resources, etc.). Further, staff members commonly have skills and experience that are not limited to their current role; in such situations, developing an internal register of staff skills may be useful. Bringing in a staff person from a different programme who has the relevant skills is also a way of encouraging the sharing of experience and learning across an organisation.

When considering an internal consultancy, it is important to establish whether the work can be delivered with the degree of independence required by the particular situation. For example, some donors will require external consultants for evaluation exercises, or at least for leadership of the team. An alternative might be to commission staff of a similar organisation (working in the same area), perhaps as part of a sharing of experience and learning. This arrangement is sometimes called *peer review*, or *peer support*. A person of similar status, working for a similar organisation, may provide greater independence than an internal staff member. He or she will have some local knowledge and understanding, but not as much internal knowledge as a genuine insider.

Single consultant or team?

Does the assignment require a single person, or is it so big and complex that it requires a range of skills that could be better provided by several people working together? If the work will span several countries, it may be necessary to have a number of separate teams, with some form of central co-ordination.

Working as a solo consultant can be very lonely and lead to a narrow approach. Two consultants could give more breadth to the work. The second person could be entirely managed by the lead consultant, through a form of subcontracting which would avoid increasing the management load for the client.

> '*I hire him* [a second consultant] *for just half a day to read the draft report and give me feedback on how it reads. It costs me from my fees, but the client gets a better report.*'
> (A consultant)

The use of two consultants is highly valued by consultants, but often rejected by clients on the grounds of increased costs. But two consultants working together provide a far greater range of experience and ways of working than a solo consultant. If one is male and the other female, communications may be easier, especially when conducting interviews and training sessions. Rather than making decisions solely on costs, the client should be open to the suggestion of bringing in another consultant for part or all of the assignment.

Freelance consultants or consultancy companies?

The client should consider whether to hire a solo self-employed consultant or a consultancy company. A whole range of organisations provide consultancy services to the international development sector. They will either provide consultants from their core staff, or recruit them from among their associates. They can usually assemble a team on behalf of the client, thus saving the client's time. Furthermore, if an individual consultant cannot complete an assignment for any reason, the company should be able to provide a suitable substitute. Companies usually provide a guarantee of quality, and the higher cost of consultants sourced through companies should be offset against this fact.

National or international experience?

What is the ideal balance of international versus national experience? Consultants who have worked in a range of countries may be able to bring wider experience and greater understanding of donors' concerns. For some assignments a consultant can do a good job without detailed local knowledge. Many development initiatives in different contexts address very similar issues, and an experienced consultant without local knowledge may be able to play a key role in identifying the issues and providing judgement and comparisons with other situations, while locally specific knowledge could be provided by another team member.

> 'We only hire international consultants if (the skills) are not available locally; we normally hire nationals. The only exception is if we do an independent evaluation and the person is bringing in knowledge and learning from elsewhere; the international consultant should either know the region or team up with a national consultant.'
> (A client)

Familiarity with your organisation?

Understanding the client's work and organisational culture can be a major advantage, and consultants who know how things are done, as well as what is done, will initially make progress more quickly. This quality should not be overvalued, however, because the range of potential consultants will be narrower, and a quick start is not always the most important consideration. And after a while the advantage of familiarity may be offset by an increasing lack of independence. It might be better to plan to take more time and invest in the induction of a consultant who is new to the organisation.

Key qualifications and competencies

Consultancies in international development, particularly in such fields as natural-resources management, civil-society capacity building, nutritional assessment, business development, trade policy, and advocacy and lobbying, obviously need an appropriate level of technical skills or expertise. But such skills are not sufficient in themselves: technical experts work in contexts that require a participatory approach and the inclusion of stakeholders. This demands an understanding of power dynamics, and the sensitivity to ensure that the views of women and other often excluded groups are heard.

Specialists need practical experience of applying their expertise in consultancy situations. If they are primarily academics, are they likely to use the consultancy to pursue their own research? And will they be able to adopt a practical approach to the work?

> *'I advised the team against contracting an academic anthropologist. However, they did. Unfortunately the person never produced any useful work, but after many months he came back with hundreds of tapes useful for his own research!'*
> (A manager)

Other essential skills

Languages

What languages are required, and at what level? Can interpreters be used, if the consultant does not have the ideal language skills? Will it be necessary to manage large meetings in the local language, or to hold complex and formal discussions with contacts at different levels? Managing meetings with high-level government officials requires different language skills from engaging in one-to-one discussions with local village elders or marginalised community members.

Writing skills

In many consultancy assignments, the written report is seen as the ultimate product of the work. The report may have to serve a range of purposes. How important are good writing skills for the exercise in question? What language or languages are required for written documents? Is it possible to hire a translator or a skilled editor to improve a rough draft produced by a consultant who otherwise has all the skills necessary to do the job?

Consider the needs of the users of the documents. Sympathetic partners or a purely internal readership may tolerate a less polished style of writing or presentation. Officials in government departments may be more critical and require a formal style if they are to take the content of the report seriously. Internal references in a report intended for the public domain will almost certainly need to be explained in a glossary in order to make them comprehensible. It might not be realistic to expect one single report to meet the needs of all the stakeholders involved.

Sensitive interviewing skills

Consultants should be capable of conducting interviews sensitively. Staff of international development agencies often have a high degree of personal involvement in their work, and they may perceive evaluation questions as personally threatening. Particular skills may be necessary when assessing an emergency response. Staff may have done their best under very difficult circumstances, and probing questions may be perceived as absurd or insulting.

With people who have been severely traumatised, conventional forms of interviewing or participatory work may not be appropriate at all. In such circumstances the consultant needs specialist interviewing and counselling skills, and appropriate conditions need to be put in place to enable interviewees to feel secure. The consultants should also be alert to situations where people might be putting themselves at risk simply by talking to visiting consultants.[8]

Shared values

As we have seen, an easy understanding between consultant and client is considered very important by both parties. Kubr[9] emphasises the importance of rapport, suggesting that if there were only one criterion to be applied, this would be the most reliable to use.

Other criteria

A balanced team

It is important to ensure that there is an appropriate gender balance in the team, especially for assignments which require consultations with men and women in local communities. Local culture may require women to be interviewed by women; women in any case may prefer to talk to women (and men may prefer to be interviewed by men). Similarly, young people and older people may prefer interviews with people of their own age. A mix of nationalities and ethnic origins may also be appropriate. There are no fixed rules; but where the quality of interviews can determine the success of a consultancy, it is essential to take such factors into consideration when building a consultancy team.

Professional integrity, code of conduct, guarantee of work

Clients should be sure that the consultant whom they choose will behave in a professional and ethical manner. This relates to conflicts of interest, confidentiality of material, and appropriate behaviour within the client organisation and with its partners. It helps if the consultant has been recommended by trusted contacts, but the client should always ask prospective consultants if they have a statement of principles, or code of conduct, to which they adhere. This may be a set of standards prescribed by a particular professional body, or a personal statement by the individual consultant. A code of conduct may help to make clear how a consultant intends to manage his or her work and relationships. In particular it may include a commitment not to undertake work for which he or she is not professionally competent.[10] See Chapter 12 for a detailed discussion of ethical issues.

Professional competence

Much information about basic qualifications and experience can be obtained by a careful scrutiny of the consultant's CV or statement of capability. When a consultancy company is being assessed, the client needs to be sure that the individuals who are being proposed as candidates will not later be replaced by less experienced substitutes. It is wise to include a relevant clause in any contract, to prevent this happening.

Ability to deliver

Trying to do several jobs at the same time is often a major problem for freelance consultants who work alone. The client should explain the timetable and ask the consultant for a realistic assessment of his or her availability to complete the work. This is a difficult issue, and some flexibility may be required on both sides in order to reach an acceptable timetable. When a company is being considered, and much of the management and logistics is being entrusted to it, the client needs to be sure that the company has the capacity and systems to deal with the assignment, particularly one that involves international work and complex multi-country studies.

Approach to the work / proposed design

In formal selection procedures, consultants will have to provide a general written description of how they will do the work, even if it is not possible to provide every detail. This submission will be complemented by discussions during interviews and negotiations. Even in more informal selection processes, it is worthwhile for clients to ask consultants to describe how they will approach the work. The Terms of Reference could be used as the starting point for this discussion. It is helpful to have the ToR presented in writing, to minimise the danger of misunderstanding, and to confirm that there is a shared understanding of approach. It should be possible to assess the extent to which the consultant has understood the task in hand, is offering something better than other candidates, and is proposing a realistic and cost-conscious way of doing the work.

Cost

The negotiation of fees is one of the most difficult aspects of commissioning a consultancy, and it is particularly difficult for relatively inexperienced solo consultants. See Chapter 9 for a detailed discussion of how fees are calculated and negotiated.

In many formal selection procedures, a statement of the estimated costs of the consultancy is sent in a separate sealed envelope and assessed by people who are not the ones responsible for assessing the main proposal. Although organisations need to consider costs carefully, cost should not be the single most important criterion. Furthermore, when considering complete budgeted proposals, it is important to understand the reasons why costings differ between proposals. For example: is one firm using more inexperienced – and therefore cheaper – consultants? What is the daily rate underlying the proposal? Are some elements included in the ToR that could be done equally well by internal staff of the client organisation?

For each particular consultancy, clients will choose specific criteria for search and selection, but the information presented here should indicate the kinds of thing to consider. It is common for criteria to be categorised as either 'essential' or 'desirable'.

Sources of consultants

General information about consultancy services can be found through professional associations, local chambers of commerce, and searches on the Internet. However, NGO networks and people and contacts in similar organisations are the best starting point.

Consultancy registers / databases

Representative bodies of the NGO sector in a particular country may keep registers of organisations and individuals that provide services. Many organisations working in the development sector hold their own databases of consultants. In simple terms, individual managers might keep files on people whom they have previously hired; or an organisation might maintain fairly sophisticated electronic databases that are periodically updated. These are most useful if there are clear criteria for defining who will be entered in the database. Sometimes managers receive unsolicited CVs and marketing information from individuals and firms which they may store on file and take out when the time comes to search for a suitable consultant.

Anyone considering developing a database or already operating one should be aware of the legal implications of maintaining it, and in particular any data-protection laws which may restrict the type of information that is held, and the use that is made of it. Data-protection law may give people the right to see what is held under their names on the database. This means that a client must be able to justify negative or controversial comments and be prepared to share them with the consultant concerned if he or she exercises the right to challenge them.

In recent years a number of Internet-based databases have been developed, containing the details of thousands of potential consultants. Individuals may register with them free of charge, while companies and organisations have to pay a subscription to sign up. The databases may be linked to commercial enterprises or to donor-funded networks, such as DevelopmentEx (www.developmentex.com); Siyanda, with a particular focus on gender (www.siyanda.com); and ALNAP, with a particular focus on humanitarian work (www.alnap.org). Sites like these enable clients to search for consultants within a large international pool; but of course clients still need to investigate the competence and appropriateness of the consultants.

Consultancy companies

A wide range of companies provide consultancy services for the international development sector. They range from the major inter-national management-consultancy firms with local representatives around the world to smaller, locally based groups that may be focused on a particular sector. In some cases the local consultancy market has developed in response to the demands of donors. In the UK in recent years, several organisations have been established to provide specific services to the sector; for example, they evaluate emergency operations, provide support for monitoring and evaluation systems, and offer training on conflict resolution, organisational development, and capacity building in administration and management.

Advertising through print or electronic media

Clients can advertise their search for a consultant via traditional press and electronic media, either through their own organisation's website, if it has a page for job opportunities, or by advertising through the websites of other organisations or networks (for example, MandE News at www.mande.co.uk/news.htm).

Personal contacts

Many consultants are hired through personal contacts and networks. In our interviews, clients said that they relied to a great extent on personal networks and individual recommendations to find consultants; and consultants said that they got almost all their work through their networks of contacts.

Networks of personal contacts may produce consultants who have already been used successfully; or consultants who are known to the client, though never used; or consultants who have been recommended by other people in the client organisation, by colleagues in sister organisations, by people whom the client respects professionally, or by other stakeholders in the work. If a potential consultant is identified by two or more of these different sources of advice, the client may feel reasonably confident of having found a reliable consultant.

The amount of work that a client should invest in the search for a consultant or consultancy team should be proportional to the importance or size of the job. One of the reasons why clients rely on direct contacts to find consultants is that it is cheap and quick, and it may be hard to justify investing in a more elaborate process for a very small contract.

The disadvantages of using personal contacts are that this method of recruitment does not allow equal opportunities, and it restricts the options to those who are already known, or already connected to those who are known. Consequently the organisation is not bringing in new experience and expanding the diversity of its consultants. The pressure to recruit quickly often means that the use of personal links is the only effective method available; but a consultant may be selected for being available, instead of for being the best possible person for the job.

Since the success of consultancy depends largely on the relationship between the consultant and the client, it is always tempting to use known consultants, but a better solution to the problems described above is to allow more time for planning the assignment and inducting new consultants to the organisation, and in developing understanding between the client and the consultant.

8 | Assessing consultants

This chapter describes initial negotiations between clients and prospective consultants. Then it presents a process for using expressions of interest and tenders when a more formal selection procedure is required.

It is always preferable to hold interviews as part of a selection process, and this is particularly true in consultancy, where the relationship between client and consultant is so important. But interviews are not always feasible: the prospective consultant may be in a different country from the client; interviews take time, and clients are often in a hurry; often there is no budget to cover the costs of the recruitment process; and the consultant may be reluctant to invest time in an interview if there is no guarantee of work. An interview is ideal for establishing the relationship and enabling the client to assess whether or not the consultant's style of working is appropriate, in addition to assessing the skills and experience that they bring to the work. Nevertheless, it is common for consultants to be recruited at a distance, on the basis of a CV alone. The ease of communication by e-mail now makes it possible to obtain answers to questions, even when an interview is not possible.

> 'You rarely get all the attributes that you would ideally like. Therefore
> it is important to get a balance and not expect consultants to do things
> beyond their competence or experience.'
> (A client)

The CV

The curriculum vitae (CV) remains an important tool in the selection of consultants. Consultants should have a range of CVs ready at all times and be prepared to provide an appropriate version to clients as soon as they are contacted.

There seems to be no standard format in use in the NGO sector. Clients can help by explaining what they want to know, and what type of document they would find most helpful. Consultants probably need to keep on file at least three formats of their CV: one short version, summarising their experience (no longer than two pages); one longer one, arranged in chronological order; and one arranged according to skills and sectoral experience (two pages only). They should update their CVs after each piece of work.

CVs are difficult to interpret if they do not make clear the role that the consultant played. For example, *'Evaluation of X programme in Y place'* may mean that the consultant designed and led the whole consultancy; but it could mean that he or she simply had the job of writing up part of the findings from notes provided by the project leader.

A CV records the quantity of consultancies undertaken, and therefore the consultant's range of experience; but crucial information about the quality of the work and the degree to which the client was satisfied with it is not usually evident from a CV. However, repeated commissions from the same client are likely to indicate satisfactory performances.

Taking up references

Taking up references is standard practice in staff recruitment, and it should be so in the hiring of consultants. The common use of personal networks to identify consultants means that there has already been a recommendation from a known person, which constitutes a reference in itself; but when a shortlist is drawn up, it is reasonable to ask a candidate for a second opinion in the form of an independent reference. Consultants should be able to nominate appropriate people to speak on their behalf at a moment's notice.

When taking up references, clients should prepare their questions with care, and listen to the answers with great attention. Note that some referees will respond only to written requests. This is a helpful practice, because it obliges the client to be precise, and it gives the referee a clear brief and time to compose a careful reply.

Recommending consultants

If asked to recommend a consultant, you should describe actual work that is known to you, and avoid a more general discussion of the consultant's skills. Be clear about the basis of your remarks, and give precise information about what the person did well or less well in the situation that you know about. If a consultancy has not gone well, it could be that there were mitigating factors of which you are not aware.

Note also that putting people in touch with each other is not the same as providing a reference. Through their professional networks, many consultants know a large number of other consultants by reputation; but they may not have direct knowledge of the quality of their work. When asked for suggestions, it is important to state clearly whether you are simply passing on information, or actually making a recommendation.

Examples of previous work

The ability to write clearly is one of the most important skills that a consultant needs, because almost all consultancies require the production of a report, which will probably be used for a variety of purposes. In principle it is good practice to ask to see examples of consultants' previous work. In fact, this is rarely done, perhaps partly because it is difficult to know what constitutes proof of ability. A report or document might be a genuine piece of work by the candidate, or it might be something that they were only slightly involved with. Another problem is that the legal ownership of relevant reports is almost always vested with the client. Copyright laws and fear of the exposure of internal business may make clients reluctant to allow reports to be used by consultants after a consultancy is finished. Consultants should collect material that can legitimately be used to demonstrate their ability to write. These should be texts of which they are clearly the author, the content of which would not embarrass any person or institution associated with the work.

If the report needs to be written in a language other than the first language of the consultant, the client should take extra care to assess the consultant's writing skills before the contract is agreed. Alternatively the client should consider allowing the consultant to write in his or her first language, and make provision for translation and editing support. This would be a better solution than losing the quality of the consultant's work in a poorly written report.

Contacting consultants

The use of e-mail has transformed the first contacts between clients and consultants and has almost entirely replaced telephone calls. E-mail benefits clients, because they can send an initial message to a range of consultants at the same time, very economically. It also benefits consultants, because it gives them time to study the proposition and look through their diary of engagements before replying. If contacted by telephone, a consultant should not feel obliged to give an immediate response, but may request further information and agree a convenient time to return the phone call if he or she needs time to reflect on the proposal.

The first contact should include a very brief overview of the work that is likely to be involved in the assignment, together with an ideal timetable. The client should also explain how contact has been made with the consultant, if that is not already clear.

Initial scouting

The process in which the consultant and the client explore the possibilities of working together is sometimes called *scouting*. It is useful to give this part of the process a name – at least to acknowledge that it exists and that it involves negotiations. These initial negotiations are important and are unlike the process by which other recruitments are made. Scouting permits both parties to modify their offers and negotiate in a more open way than is the case with a formal recruitment.

When a consultant first hears of a possible job, he or she needs to make a number of quick assessments:

- *Am I interested in the work?*
- *Am I available?*
- *Can I do the job well?*

If the answers to these questions are positive, at least in principle, the consultant sends a CV, and the client sends the ToR. In the early stages of negotiating the consultancy, there will probably be many variable factors to consider, and the process requires a lot of work and time to get right. The consultant and client are testing each other out and assessing their abilities to work together well. It is helpful if both sides acknowledge that it is a negotiation, and that each may have to compromise in order to reach a satisfactory resolution. It will be easier to develop a relationship of trust if there is a sense of reciprocity in the exchanges of information. Clients should make it clear if they are in contact with several potential consultants; consultants should explain something about the competing demands on their time. Both sides will need to set limits to the scouting negotiations and agree the point at which they will make a commitment or stop trying.

Box 8.1: Interviewing candidates for consultancy work

These are the kinds of question that you might ask:

- Would you be interested in taking on this work (or, Would you be interested in submitting a tender for the work, based on the written brief)?
- Are you available on the dates or in the period required?
- What kind of work have you done before that is relevant to this training or consultancy?
- What approach would you take to this work?
- What relevant skills or expertise do you have?
- What values or principles underpin your work?
- How do you demonstrate your commitment to equality of opportunity?
- Would you do it alone, or with others? If with others, how will you choose your associates?
- What are your systems for quality assurance? How do you review and evaluate your work?
- What are your fees for work of this type? Can you estimate your likely expenses?
- If we want to have a pre-meeting with you before deciding whether to hire you, would you charge for this meeting and/or for travel costs?
- Can you provide further written information about yourself?
- Can you provide referees for similar work you have done?

(From Management Development Network: 'Choosing a Consultant'[11])

Some consultants say that scouting meetings should be paid for at normal consultancy rates. There is some justification for this, if the consultant is helping the client to think through the work and define the approach and methodology. However, for most scouting meetings both sides want to keep their options open and meet without obligation on either side. Consultants expect to invest some unpaid work in the process of exploring work opportunities, but clients cannot expect consultants to give unlimited amounts of time to discussions. Consultants should politely tell clients that they are happy to go on discussing the details of the work, but they have reached the point where they have to 'set the meter running'. Most consultants are willing to give approximately one day of work, free of charge, to the pursuit of a potential contract. Clients should ask consultants how much time they will be willing to go on giving if the scouting seems to be taking a long time.

The person conducting the scouting on behalf of the client organisation should tell the candidate the identity of the person(s) who will actually be responsible for commissioning and managing the consultancy.

Availability

Getting the timing right is probably the biggest problem faced by consultants in international development. The question of availability (*'Will you be available at X time?'*) is often not as clear-cut as it seems. For one thing, timetables tend to slip and can usually be rearranged if necessary. Most solo consultants are likely to be busy in the short term, but even very successful consultants may not be certain about their commitments more than a few months in advance.

> *'A client called me up and said "Anyone who is any good is booked up ages in advance, but I thought you might be available". They actually said this! I don't think they realised what they were saying.'*
> (A consultant)

> *'This is the first year (out of eight years spent in consulting work) when I have known what I will be doing for a whole year in advance.'*
> (A consultant)

A further complication is that consultants cannot afford to take on assignments that are back-to-back: they need time between contracts to rest and to attend to routine administrative tasks. International travel takes people away from their families and offices; it is tiring; it often leads to periods of sickness. People need a break between assignments that require a lot of travel in difficult conditions.

Clients need to be aware that consultants are making this kind of calculation as they try to assess their availability. For example, a contract of fifteen days' work may occupy a consultant for a month. However well a consultant tries to plan, problems frequently occur when one contract is delayed or another is brought forward, reducing the time for concluding work on the first assignment, then resting, and then preparing for the next.

The difficulties of managing the timing are greater for solo consultants than for consultants working for an agency. Freelancers will be juggling several requests from several clients and they are likely to commit themselves to the first client who offers a firm commission.

Interesting work

Consultants are likely to be attracted to work about which they already have good knowledge and in which they have some experience. However, the most interesting work might be something that seems largely familiar but also contains some elements that are new and challenging. For example, the consultant might be asked to do work that she or he has done before, but in a new place. If a client is trying to attract a particular consultant who appears to be reluctant, it may be helpful to explore the opportunities for learning that the assignment presents, and explain why it might be interesting.

Competencies

It is a matter of some concern that the assessment of consultants' competencies largely depends on self-assessment by the consultants, and simple questioning – on the basis of a CV – by the clients. It is the responsibility of consultants to be honest about their suitability for a particular piece of work; and it is the responsibility of the client to describe the work accurately. In most situations the solution lies in the degree to which the exchanges between them are frank and open. A responsible consultant can make the situation easier by disclosing his or her doubts, but will find this difficult to do without feeling confident or at ease with the client. The responsible client will also behave in an open way, so that the exchanges allow the two sides to learn enough about the proposed assignment, and the necessary skills, to reach an informed, shared decision. See Chapter 12 for discussion of ethical concerns.

In summary, consultants are likely to want to take work that fulfils the following criteria (presented in no particular order).

- It appears to be interesting in itself and could lead to learning for the consultant.
- It may lead the consultant into new places or new sectors, or to working with new clients, with the prospect of extending his or her experience.
- It will be straightforward and has simple management relationships.
- It seems well considered and is clearly owned by the client.
- It appears likely to have a useful impact on the lives of poor people.
- It has clear, fixed dates attached to it.
- It involves people whom they think they can understand easily and work well with.
- It will be properly paid (in terms of fees, expenses, and the timing of payments).

Negotiations

After the initial scouting, the negotiations will continue on the basis that there is a possibility that the client and consultant will work together. The consultant should try to find out the following information: the real timetable; the history behind the proposal; the identity of the key client; the identities of the stakeholders; and the terms and conditions.

The consultant needs to know when the work should ideally be done, and what scope there might be for changes. The client needs to present the reasoning behind the ideal calendar and explain how the assignment fits with other work. The consultant will also want to understand the context, the origins of the consultancy, and the identity of the person who has been responsible for managing the process so far. Is the work already tightly defined, or is it still being thought through – in which case, is the consultant required to play a role in developing the ToR further?

Fees, expenses, and other conditions

We have found it common for people working in the NGO sector to feel uncomfortable haggling over money; consultants may fear that they will be seen as greedy if they argue over fees or costs. Some cultures accept robust arguments over money, but for some people it is deeply embarrassing. This can make it harder to conclude an open negotiation on terms that satisfy both sides. Discussing money is the second most difficult problem, after getting the timing right, for the consultants who took part in our survey.

The most important element of financial negotiations is the question of whether to pay a daily rate or a lump sum for the contract. It may take some time to make the calculations that determine the overall worth of a contract. For these reasons, it may be helpful to conduct the negotiations in two steps. It should be possible to break off talking about the terms and conditions and allow each side to do some calculations before holding a second round of talks and reaching a conclusion. E-mail exchanges allow this kind of reflection. Both sides should feel able to ask for time to reconsider if they are negotiating by telephone or face to face. See Chapter 9 for a detailed discussion of how to calculate consultancy fees.

Consultants will want to know the client's policy on expenses. There may be scope for negotiating modifications in order to improve the conditions of the contract for the consultant. In most cases the arrangements for expenses are not likely to determine the acceptance or rejection of an offer of work.

Before starting negotiations, the client needs to know how much money is available for paying the consultant(s), and the degree of flexibility permitted when arranging the methods of payment. The consultant needs to define an acceptable daily rate, or a range of rates which specifies the lowest acceptable figure. Successful and rapid negotiations may depend on the scope for altering daily rates, or for switching from a rate calculated by the day to an agreed fee for the job. The negotiations may seem one-sided, in the sense that the client is only discussing a budget, while the consultant is discussing his or her livelihood. In fact, the balance of power in the negotiations depends on how urgently the client needs a consultant and how desperately the consultant needs work.

Deciding to go forward

The result of the initial contact is no more than a decision on whether or not to continue the negotiations in an attempt to reach more detailed contractual agreements on the specifics of the consultancy.

This relationship will work

A successful conclusion to negotiations is an agreed contract and ToR. Both parties will have done a risk assessment (however informally), to check whether they feel that the relationship is likely to work well enough to get the work done effectively.

If the consultant decides not to proceed, he or she almost always receives a request for names of other people who might be interested. Most consultants are happy to supply such information. It can be seen as part of the bargain, which might one day lead to a direct offer of work. Clients should ask consultants if they mind being asked for recommendations. It is important also to make it clear at the beginning of the conversation that this might be what you have in mind.

> 'Sometimes people ask me if I am interested in work that they must know I cannot do and then they quickly ask if I can recommend someone else. It would be better if they just asked me directly for recommendations.'
> (A consultant)

It can be disheartening to be asked many times for contact details by clients who have never hired you. It feels as though they are only interested in your address book!

Should the work be postponed?

All recruitment starts off as the search for the ideal person or the ideal team. During the process it becomes a search for the optimum person: that is, the best available person from those who have presented themselves. It is necessary to accept that all the attributes and qualities described in the invitation may not be available in the best candidates, and that compromises must be made. Making compromises is not easy, and, while checklists and scoring grids are helpful, eventually the manager of the process has to take a risk.

When a client is finding it difficult to identify the right person, it may become necessary to choose between adhering to the timetable or delaying the work in order to get the best person/team for the job. It is usually possible to reorganise the work so that the right consultants can be used. Alternatively it may be better to organise a limited assignment, instead of the original consultancy: aiming, for example, to confirm the diagnosis of the client, or to design a more detailed consultancy that could be carried out at another time. This kind of input may be very valuable and could save a lot of money in the long run.

Tenders

Calling for tenders

If the consultancy work will be extensive and complex, it may be best to use a team, and to select the team by competitive tenders. A tender is a formal proposal from a consultant or consultancy group to carry out a piece of work. A formal tendering process may be required by the client organisation's policies if the value of the work exceeds certain budgetary levels.

A tendering process involves at least four steps: advertisements or invitations to tender; review of tenders; interviews; and appointment of the consultancy team. Sometimes the process starts by calling for expressions of interest (EoIs), reviewing the results, and then inviting a shortlist of three–five of the respondents to submit full tenders.

One advantage of the competitive tendering process is that it inspires confidence by being more open and transparent than the use of personal networks. One disadvantage is that the tendering will add at least one month to the recruitment of consultants, and there is no realistic way of shortening this period. If the consultancy input has to start within two months, it is probably already too late to use a tendering process. Larger international development bodies require companies to go through a process of pre-qualification before they are allowed to submit bids for tenders. Once qualified, the company can bid for a range of contracts.

Solo consultants find it harder than consultancy groups to form teams for specific pieces of work. This may be because it is harder for them to find the time, unpaid, to develop bids and to sign up other solo consultants who can guarantee to be available at the end of the uncertain tendering process. In fact this uncertainty exists for all agencies, and some groups of solo consultants successfully bid for larger contracts. They are usually groups who have some history of working together, and shared levels of trust.

The tender process is set out in the call for tenders, and the setting of a calendar makes for a rigorously defined sequence of events. It is therefore very important to state whether or not the process will be open to suggestions for changes and the input of ideas from the consultants.

Contents of a Call for Tenders

A Call for Tenders may make specific reference to some points that are contained in the ToR. Candidates may be invited to show how they would meet the ToR and carry out the work. The invitation should briefly describe the background to the assignment: the reasons why the organisation is commissioning this piece of work now, and also perhaps why it seems appropriate to use external consultants. It should make explicit reference to particular policies that apply to the entire work of the organisation: for example, some agencies are obliged to recruit people of certain nationalities or from agencies registered in certain countries. It is wise to mention organisational policies like gender equality or environmental sustainability, if these are likely to be important criteria, so that candidates can take account of them when preparing their bids.

The tender invitation will normally contain instructions on how candidates should present their proposal, including the names of the team members and their credentials. It is important to know who will be involved, and how their skills will be used. An indicative programme of work makes it easy for the client to understand the bid, especially if it shows who will be involved, and for what periods of time in the different stages of the consultancy. This allows more detailed questioning during the interview, to explore how the tasks will be achieved and what skills will be used. The client needs to feel confident that the consultants mentioned in the tender-bid document will be the people who will actually do the work. It is known for consultant companies to win bids but then provide other staff to carry out the work. This is why confirmation-of-availability forms are used, although they are not an absolute guarantee that any particular consultant will actually be available.

Box 8.2: A Call for Tenders – sample table of contents[12]

Terms of reference
Estimate of the volume of work
Financial limit
Required structure of the proposal
Period of validity of the offer
Deadline and format for the submission
Formal terms and conditions of contract
Preferred basis of remuneration
References to be provided
Need for confidentiality
Selection criteria and process
Contact point for queries
Special conditions
Request for CVs and details of experience

The question of costs should be dealt with directly, in order to save time and work on both sides. It may be necessary to do no more than state which costs will be met, and what arrangements will be made for subsistence and incidental expenses. These items are not likely to influence the total cost of the project by very much, and a couple of lines of text will avoid discussions about what is not normally negotiable: for example, economy air fares, *per diem* rates, local travel, hotel costs, and so on.

A Call for Tenders should include a description of how the tender-selection process will be managed. It should give closing dates, interview dates, and ideal start and finish dates, including any fixed dates. It should also make it clear how additional information could be obtained from the client.

Tender invitations should give an indication of the budget, or a suggestion of the expected scope by indicating the time allocated to different parts of the work, to enable consultants to design a meaningful tender document.

> *'When we looked at the proposed budget, we thought it wasn't worth submitting a tender. Our proposal was more than twice the budget they had proposed! However, we did submit and we won the tender. The client realised that we were proposing to do a thorough piece of work.'*
> (A consultant)

Asking for additional information

Consultants will always take up an invitation to gather more information about the work for which they are bidding. Any additional information is likely to help them to target their proposals more accurately.

In the case of large commercial tenders or tenders for the major development agencies, there are strict rules that forbid canvassing. Contact between those who are tendering and those who will judge the tenders is formally prohibited. The Call for Tenders must be extremely clear about the type of contact and exchange of information that is acceptable. A client will often decide that any answers to queries requested by one group will be circulated to all those who are submitting tenders. It is usual to state a cut-off point for information requests, about 10–14 days before the deadline for submission of tender documents. Sometimes clients will hold a joint briefing with shortlisted tenderers at the beginning of the tender process, in order to give more information about the proposal and to answer queries, thus reducing the risk of misdirected proposals and wasted effort on all sides.

Taking part in several competing bids

An individual consultant may be asked by competing teams to be associated with their tenders for a piece of work. Some consulting groups and some development aid agencies insist that members of the tender bids should sign exclusive commitments of availability; this means in theory that the consultant who signs the statement can take part in only a single bid. However, there is no consistency among organisations that require statements of exclusive availability, and it is not obvious that there is any advantage to the clients or to the consultants in demanding them. The only incentive for requiring such statements seems to apply to the group who are making the tender, if they can claim the exclusive use of a particular person's skills and experience.

Two-step tenders

The use of 'expressions of interest' (EoIs) is a way of allowing a two-step process in order to reduce the effort invested in developing unsuccessful bids, and the time spent in reviewing bids. For consultants this is particularly important, since the time spent in preparing tenders is unpaid. Calls for expressions of interest could be done by routine advertising, or a number of pre-qualified agencies could be contacted directly and invited to submit an EoI. After shortlisting has been done on the basis of the EoIs, a small number of contenders, commonly between three and five, are asked to submit more detailed bids. This is similar to the way in which donors can ask for short 'outline' proposals before inviting full proposals for funding.

Assessing tenders

Tenders are assessed in order to decide whom to interview. The tender document will allow the client to assess the main elements of the team's approach to the work – which may be more important than the actual details of the separate tasks. It is important for the client to feel at ease with the approach that the consulting team will use, and to be confident that they have the skills to adapt work as needed in order to achieve desired results.

The tender document should set out the track record of the company or group of consultants, and the skills and experience of the main members of the team. It is helpful to the client to know if the consultants have previous experience of working together on similar assignments. This is the best indicator of their chances of adjusting to the specific circumstances of the commission in question.

Clients usually ask consulting agencies to provide statements of availability for each member of the team. Such statements may make it easier for the agency to put pressure on a particular consultant to carry out the work, but they would probably not have any force in a legal dispute. The problem is the lack of reciprocity: the consultant is being asked to make a commitment to doing a piece of work, but the consulting group cannot offer any commitment in return, since they have not yet won the contract.

Receiving and assessing bids

The individuals in the client organisation who are drawn together to form the panel to assess the bids and interview successful consultants should be properly briefed so that they can make informed decisions. Common reasons for rejecting bids include the following.

- The consultancy team lacks relevant skills and experience in the area required (either technical, geographical, or sectoral).
- The task is too big or complex for the resources of the consultants.
- No distinctive features make the bid stand out from others.
- The bid fails to provide requested information in the required format.
- The quoted price is far above that of other bidders, or significantly above the available budget.[13]

Note that there is no legal obligation to accept the lowest bid, or any particular bid. The lowest bid may not be the best in terms of value, for it could be that the bidder has underestimated the complexity of the exercise.

It is good practice to provide feedback if it is requested by those whose tenders are not accepted.

9 | Costing a consultancy – and other financial matters

This chapter discusses the practicalities of costing a consultancy, including the question of fees and expenses paid to consultants. As noted in Chapter 8, some staff in non-profit organisations feel uncomfortable when they have to negotiate such things. This chapter explains how to calculate fees and realistic costs.

> 'It's easier to discuss rates with a commercial company than with NGOs. Companies tend to be clear about what they have to pay and what they are prepared to pay.'
> (A consultant)

Preliminary estimates

In the interests of good financial management and accountability, at the early stages of considering a consultancy clients should assess how much the exercise is likely to cost. The first item to be assessed should be consultants' fees, which are likely to be the largest item in the budget. There will be costs to pay for items such as travel, meetings, translators, visas, and administrative and logistical support. The cost of using internal organisational resources should not be forgotten – for example:

- management time: identifying and hiring consultants, dealing with the consultants once hired, monitoring progress, ensuring that payments are made;
- time spent by operational staff in briefing the consultants and taking part in review exercises or interviews;
- administrative support: if a staff person is allocated to the exercise, there may be costs in hiring temporary support to replace him or her for the duration of the exercise;

- resources such as vehicles, which will be unavailable for normal use while supporting the consultancy;
- potential costs of implementing any recommendations resulting from the work.

A preliminary estimate of the costs of a consultancy will enable clients to judge if the necessary resources are available, before they invest any more time in the proposition. A clear view of the overall costs will also help in assessing consultants' proposals. A very low estimate may mean that the consultant has not appreciated the scope of the exercise. On the other hand, an estimate that is higher than the client's provisional budget may mean that the client has not taken full account of the needs of the study.

Estimating the budget will help clients to judge the worth of the exercise in terms of expected benefits; clarify if there is enough money in existing budgets to cover the expected costs, or whether extra money needs to be raised; and ensure that they comply with any organisational policies or national regulations in terms of tendering processes. (For example, in some organisations purchases worth more than a certain sum will require the manager to call for bids from at least three suppliers.)

Calculating fees

Fees can be calculated in several different ways, and the appropriate basis may be the subject of negotiation with the consultant.

Table 9.1: Fees and billing methods	
Time-based fee	The client is charged for all the time spent on the assignment. (This is often preferred by consultants in the commercial sector.)
Lump sum/flat fee	The client and consultant negotiate a clearly defined upper limit on what can be charged in return for the defined outputs/deliverables.
Fee contingent on results	The fee is related to the achievement of the quantifiable results specified in the assignment.
Percentage fee	The fee is calculated as a percentage of the total project costs.
Retainer fee	A fixed amount is paid in each period for services as and when they are required.

NGOs commonly pay for consultancy with a lump-sum fee, calculated on the basis of a particular daily rate. If the consultant overruns the schedule, particularly when writing the final report, the cost of the excess will be borne by the consultant. The consultant will receive, for example, three days' fees regardless of whether they spend two days or six days on the job. Therefore consultants who have accepted a lump-sum arrangement are likely to be very sensitive to any increases in the workload that develop during the course of the consultancy.

Negotiating consultancies would be easier if there were generally agreed norms related to rates of pay and ways of working. It would be helpful if there were greater transparency about the basis for consultants' daily fee rates; common standards to determine what expenses are routinely paid for by the client and what consultants are expected to cover; and shared ideas about the time required for routine steps common to most consultancies.

The market

Most staff in client organisations whom we interviewed were unable to say on what basis their organisation had fixed its fee rates. Some agencies prescribed a maximum limit, but it was generally felt that the limits could be modified if necessary.

> '*I want to pay decent rates, but at the same time these are charity funds; I have to spend as little as I can!*'
> (A programme manager)

> '*To get IT work we use consultants, so we can go off the pay scales.*'
> (A client)

Our research suggests that fee rates do not relate to the experience of the consultant, but more typically to the client's ability to pay, or the consultant's ability to negotiate. This is reflected in the fact that consultants accept different rates from different types of client. In general, people hiring consultants would say that they set their fees according to 'the market'. We noted considerable variations within a single agency, which largely seemed to depend on the individual consultant's confidence to set a rate. There was no reference to parity with the salaries of staff of similar levels.

What consultants will accept

'What is the going daily rate for independent consultants these days? No one ever seems to complain about my rates, so maybe I am undercharging!'
(A consultant)

Consultants should work out a notional fee, based on what they need to earn each year to give them a reasonable standard of living. A comparison with the salaries of people with similar experience in client agencies may help in these calculations, taking account of the factors set out below. Of course, the responsibilities and routines of freelancers and salaried staff are different, so one cannot make a direct comparison between their levels of income; but these calculations can serve as indicators.

Having defined the level of gross income needed, the consultant will consider how many days during the year he or she would like (or needs) to work in order to achieve it. It is then possible to calculate an ideal average daily rate. In fact, the reactive nature of consultancy work tends to mean that consultants often do too much or too little work to achieve their ideal. They need to make the best of each situation, enjoying the higher income when there is too much work, and the greater leisure when there is too little.

Consultants whom we interviewed for this book reported very few occasions when they had refused work because the fees offered were too low. Similarly they did not have much experience of being rejected because the client considered their rates to be too high. Of course, a consultant may decide to accept work below his or her notional fee level if it is seen as an entry point to future work in an organisation, or a way of gaining certain experience.

Table 9.2 shows the total sums paid in fees for a range of notional daily rates (300 to 400) over contracts for different numbers of days (10 to 20). The principles of the calculations can be applied to any currency. The table shows that the total number of days is more important than the daily rate in determining the overall fees for a consultancy: increasing the daily rate from 300 to 350 for a ten-day consultancy has less impact on the total cost than increasing the number of days from 10 to 12. The client may offer a contract of ten days at 300 a day. The consultant may find it easier to agree to do the work at that rate over twelve days than to argue for a daily rate of 350. Thus the client and consultant may reach agreement on a mutually acceptable fee by making a small increase in the number of days in the contract, rather than the consultant pushing for a higher daily rate.

Table 9.2: Calculating fees – a small example

Daily rate	Number of days				
	10	12	15	17	20
300	3000	3600	4500	5100	6000
325	3250	3900	4875	5525	6500
350	3500	4200	5250	5950	7000
375	3750	4500	5625	6375	7500
400	4000	4800	6000	6800	8000

The table illustrates why it might be better for a consultant to ask for a lump sum. Suppose he or she wants to ask for 400 per day for a ten-day assignment, but the client has a budget limit of 3600 for the fees. If the consultant accepts the lump sum and works no more than nine days on the contract, he or she would appear to be receiving the preferred rate. A larger table of fee calculations is presented in Annex 6.

> 'I usually charge 600 per day for a day's training; but I don't charge for the preparation time, so I suppose my daily rate is really 300.'
> (A consultant)

A rational basis for calculating daily rates

In order to establish a more rational basis for calculating fee rates, it may be helpful to explore the differences between payments to staff and payments to consultants.

We have heard of negotiations that started on the erroneous basis of establishing a consultant's daily rate by dividing a staff member's salary by 365. This would assume that the staff member worked every day of the year and cost the employer no more than the value of his or her gross salary. But in the UK, for example, it is generally accepted that a staff person works approximately 220 days in a year after the deduction of weekends, annual leave, national holidays, and other time off such as sick leave. Moreover, the employee may spend time on training courses and a wide range of administrative tasks that are important but not part of the operational work of the organisation.

A staff member costs his or her employer between 20 and 25 per cent more than the gross salary in what are sometimes called 'on-costs'. In the UK these costs would include pension payments, national insurance contributions, medical insurance and other forms of insurance, and overheads such as heating and lighting, a place to work, and office furniture. Staff members use computers, the Internet, telephones, faxes, photocopying, stationery, and postal services. Employees may be supported by administrative staff and support staff such as IT specialists, human-resources personnel, and staff-health advisers, all of whose services could be considered part of the costs of employing the member of staff.

On the above basis, a staff member whose gross salary is equivalent to 50,000 would in reality cost his or her employer 60,000 per year. If the staff member worked on programme issues for, say, 200 days in a year, that would give a daily rate of 300. (It is possible to do the calculations in different ways by changing the numbers of days and the total salary levels.)

We can now do a similar indicative exercise to look at consultants' rates of pay. Most freelance consultants working on short-term assignments, particularly those that involve international travel, suggest that to be realistic it is difficult to achieve more than about 120 fee-earning days per year, on average. Some years they may work considerably more, and in other years they do less.

A simple way of calculating the rates of pay that a consultant should expect in order to achieve an income comparable to a staff member's annual gross income is simply to multiply the rate by the number of days worked. In Table 9.3 we set out a range of gross salary levels and then calculate the average daily rate needed to reach that level of income.

Table 9.3: 'The one-per-cent calculation' (sums rounded for clarity)				
Gross salary	40,000	50,000	60,000	70,000
Salary plus on-costs	50,000	62,000	75,000	88,000
Daily rate on 100 days	500	620	750	880
Daily rate on 120 days	420	520	625	735

Fixing the daily rate on the basis of 100 paid days per year is known as the 'one-per-cent rule'. It can be used by both consultants and clients for a very rapid assessment of an equivalence between the incomes of staff and consultants. In Table 9.3 we have used 20 per cent as the basis for assessing on-costs. This figure is likely to vary between countries.

It is important to note that the figures that emerge from these rough sums are an average figure that a consultant should achieve over a period of time, say a whole year. The consultant can therefore charge less than these rates and still achieve the same standard of living, as long as he or she also occasionally charges more than the average rate. For example, a consultant wishing to earn a similar income to that of an employee who is earning a gross annual salary of 40,000 would need an average daily fee rate of 400. It would be possible, for example, to accept work at 300/day and still reach the desired annual income if the consultant could also find work at 500/day.

A consultant has to calculate how much time is available for actual fee-earning days. Time must also be spent on obtaining assignments, networking with fellow professionals, and keeping up to date with his or her field of work. It is unlikely that time spent in getting work can be reduced, even where other investments in professional development can be postponed if necessary. Frequent international travel may entail a higher number of days' rest than the average staff person would be expected to take, and this fact should be considered in the calculations. People working in international development are exposed to higher than normal risks of sickness, and for consultants this means a consequent loss of fee-earning potential.

On top of the gross salary rate, a consultant needs to add the basic costs of running his or her business. This includes capital costs incurred in buying and maintaining essential equipment, such as a computer and printer, and running costs such as telephone rental and office supplies. Costs incurred in getting work and maintaining networks of contacts need to be added, as well as voluntary and mandatory social-security payments such as private pension contributions, national insurance payments, and private insurance to cover such things as loss of property, professional indemnity, and travel and medical insurance.

The costs of running a consultancy business for an individual freelance consultant may be similar to the on-costs shown in Table 9.3, which would make the daily rates in the table roughly appropriate. We recommend that both consultants and clients keep these calculations in mind, to enable negotiations over rates of pay to be conducted from a more objective starting point.

Calculating the time required for a consultancy

Another way to improve negotiations over fees would be to agree some norms for the time required for particular stages of the consultancy process, especially time spent on negotiating, travel, preparation, writing, training, and feedback.

Travel time is considered differently by different clients. For some it is clearly understood as part of the work; for others it is not regarded as part of the job and cannot be charged to the client. In some cases travel time can be quite significant, with a consultant taking several days to journey between his or her home base and the site of the work. This time is not always lost, since it is often used for reading, or for discussion with other consultants or staff who are travelling together. The same uncertainties can apply to very short inputs too. If a consultant travels to a nearby town for a meeting, the journey may take longer than the meeting. Should the consultant charge for attendance at the meeting and/or for the time spent away from other work? It may be useful to consider to what extent the consultant can use the time for other work. If the time spent cannot be used for other paid work, then it seems reasonable for the client to pay for the consultant's time.

Most organisations will pay for every day that a consultant is engaged on an assignment, while some will pay for only six days out of seven. They argue that people should rest for one day a week. This may be a sensible policy, especially if the assignment is longer than a couple of weeks. However, consultants who have travelled from their home base to carry out an assignment are not generally in a position to do anything else on the unpaid days. In such cases, they do not normally take rest days: they prefer to work continuously, and they will expect the total fee being offered to reflect that fact. For longer contracts, it may be helpful to stipulate a rest day.

Expenses

There are several ways in which consultants are paid to cover the costs involved in doing a piece of work. The question of what exactly is covered should be negotiated in advance between consultant and client. Table 9.4 sets out various common ways in which consultants can charge for their expenses.

Table 9.4: Methods of charging for expenses

All-inclusive fee	The fees are considered to cover all the costs involved in carrying out the work.
Fixed amount	A fixed amount is charged to cover expenses. This can be based on a percentage (10–15%) of the total fee, or a certain monetary value added to the daily fee rate.
Reimbursable expenses	Expenses (sometimes referred to as 'actuals') are claimed from the client as they are incurred. Motoring expenses tend to be charged at a set rate per mile.

In development work, different clients have different systems for paying costs, which may be *per diem*, actuals, subsistence, or a combination of these.

Per diem

A *per diem* (daily) system is probably the easiest to administer, because it is simply a daily sum of money paid to the consultant to cover costs. The consultant normally does not account for it to the client. Some organisations, such as UN agencies, have complex systems for defining daily rates in different locations to cover all expenses. In some countries (including the UK), consultants are taxed on *per diems*. In this case the consultant is advised to keep relevant receipts of expenditure that can be off-set against tax.

Actuals

The actuals system is relatively simple, in that the consultant claims the actual costs of carrying out the work. The types of expense that the consultant can claim must be clearly defined in advance. To avoid problems, it is sensible for the client to define an upper limit for reimbursable items. Often the contract states that the client will reimburse 'reasonable' expenses; interpreting what is reasonable depends on good will and an assumption of shared understanding.

Subsistence (or Daily Subsistence Allowance, DSA)

The subsistence system of payment is usually more complicated than the others, because it consists of a mixture of methods. The client may cover some costs directly and provide a sum of money to cover other costs. Subsistence arrangements will probably cover lodging, food, transport, and other expenses such as laundry.

For example, a client may pay for lodging directly and provide a sum of money for other costs, permitting the consultant to pay for food and local transport from the allowance and keep any money that is left over. In international development work, it is often the case that the client organisation is able to provide local travel far more cheaply and efficiently than other means (such as public transport or taxis). Where the client provides local travel facilities, the DSA would not need to cover it, and so the rate could be fixed at a lower level.

The contract should specify what is covered by the DSA, and whether the consultant is free to choose his or her accommodation. It may be necessary to use a phrase such as 'DSA is deemed to cover all meals and miscellaneous expenses', to make sure that the consultant does not assume that some things are covered when they are not.

The use of DSA can cause problems when the consultant cannot choose how much to spend. If, for example, the consultant is obliged to stay in a particular hotel or cannot spare the time to search out somewhere cheaper, it may prove to be impossible to cover the costs from the DSA, and the consultant will lose financially. There are good reasons for accommodation to be provided or paid for directly by the client, to enable local and international consultants to stay in the same accommodation – an arrangement which often improves their ability to work together.

Agencies that pay higher fees may pay fewer incidental costs, whereas those paying lower daily rates may in fact pay for more expenses. The most important thing is for both parties to be clear at the outset of any negotiations about what is included and what is not included.

Major expenses, such as international air travel, are often paid directly by the client organisation, because it can get cheaper deals through travel agents. Agencies based in the South who are recruiting international consultants may ask them to pay for their own international travel, and the cost is reimbursed later.

The different methods of paying for expenses involve different degrees of administrative work for the consultant and client. Subsistence payments that are accountable mean that the consultant has to collect vouchers to demonstrate expenses, and the client has to check the vouchers before making payments. Many agencies prefer to pay consultants non-accountable sums to cover costs, because this method involves much less work.

Consultants are advised to collect vouchers to show what they have spent on subsistence, partly for their own records, to keep track of their money, and partly because they may be required to produce proof of their outgoings for tax purposes. In certain situations it may be difficult to obtain receipts, so consultants may find it useful to take receipt books with them.

Below are some examples of costs that may be dealt with differently by clients.

- **Visa costs:** some agencies do not cover the costs of visas, even though a visa may be essential to getting the work done. Obtaining a visa may mean travelling to a capital city or using registered post or couriers, which may cost far more than the visa fee alone.

- **Laundry:** some agencies will not pay for laundry in hotels; others simply accept the hotel bill, including laundry charges.

- **Travel to/from the airport:** some agencies pay for public transport, and some will cover taxi fares.

- **Meals** while travelling to and from the assignment.

- **Communications:** phone calls, printing, stationery, postage, couriers, etc. These costs are sometimes reimbursed and sometimes considered to be included in the fees.

Clients may find it helpful to consider what the organisation would provide to a staff member in order to get a similar job done.

'I asked to stay in the hotel next to the office, but they said it was too costly. They put me in a cheaper hotel across town and paid for a taxi to take me to the office and back. The journey took an hour each way. It seemed a silly waste of money, and they would have got much more out of me for less if they had changed the policy on hotels.'
(A consultant)

Consultants should expect to equip themselves with the 'tools of trade' to carry out their work; they would not expect clients to provide them with computer, pens, or notebooks, for example. In certain situations where access to equipment may be difficult, some agencies will lend equipment such as laptops, water-testing kits, special communications, and security equipment. Nevertheless, consultants should expect to provide the basic tools that enable them to do the job. Special needs or extra requirements for any particular job should be discussed with the client. For example, while routine communication might be considered normal for the job, a telephone survey would cost a lot more than normal communications, and the costs involved should be covered as an additional expense.

An internal guideline for Oxfam GB staff suggests: *'fees for a consultant should include an element for general overheads that would normally occur in running a consultancy business. This would include telephone calls, stationery, photocopying, travel and subsistence in the UK.'*

Payment

For a relatively short piece of work lasting only a few days, it is acceptable for clients to defer payment until the work has been completed. For longer pieces it is usual to agree staged payments: a specified percentage of the total agreed fee on signing the contract; another percentage at a time agreed during the contract, perhaps after an interim report has been submitted; and then a final payment on completion of the assignment (most often signalled by the acceptance of a final report).

It is good practice to pay invoices promptly, and certainly within 30 days. One reason is that consultants need to build up a capital fund to tide them over periods of late payment. Payment of invoices within a reasonable length of time is of particular importance to self-employed consultants. They should not be put in the invidious position of having to ring up to ask when they are likely to be paid. Some consultants feel uncomfortable doing this.

Some consultants insist on a clause that specifies the maximum permissible delay before payment, writing on their invoices 'Terms strictly 30 days' or something similar. In practice it is virtually impossible to insist on such time limits, and clients may insert clauses in contracts allowing a delay in payments if, for example, they themselves have not been paid by their funders.

It is not always easy for a client to pay promptly if a large number of stakeholders want to comment on the consultant's report, and payment is supposed to be made after the report is found to be satisfactory. It may be possible for clients to offer payment in part if there is likely to be a long delay. Consultants could offer to amend the report without charge, or suggest that a small final payment be withheld, to allow for final revisions to be made to the report after the major part of the fee has been paid.

10 | Contracts and other legal matters

This chapter discusses legal matters: contracts, terms and conditions, and the nature of consultancy agreements.

What constitutes a contract?

Contracts are used to establish each party's rights and obligations, so that they each have a clear understanding of what is expected of them. There may be variations from one national context to another, but under English law a contract can result from any of the following: a written agreement; an oral or verbal agreement; particular behaviour or performance.

Written contracts

> 'Often the contract was cobbled together when payment was due!'
> (A member of staff)

A written contract should be agreed *before* proceeding with a consultancy, so that all parties can refer to a clear record of what has been agreed.
In its simplest form the contract should contain the following elements:

- A copy of the agreed Terms of Reference.
- Details of agreed fees and expenses.
- Confirmation of who will carry out the work (to prevent consultants substituting a less experienced person once they have won the contract).
- Details of the terms of business between the parties, including details of how payments will be made.
- A statement about the mechanism for resolving any disputes, and the jurisdiction under which any legal matters would be enforced (particularly important when people from different countries are involved in a contract).

Such a contract is not much more than a letter of agreement, and it may be sufficient for shorter pieces of work. Any subsequent changes to the agreement, for example extending the time allowed, or adjusting the Terms of Reference, should be recorded and filed with the main document. See Annex 1.

Verbal agreements

It is standard best practice to use written contracts. However, it is important to understand that verbal agreements can constitute a binding contract. Sometimes verbal agreements are made in advance of a formal written contract: in an emergency, a consultant may start work on the basis of a telephone conversation. In many cases in the international development sector, contracts are concluded by people who may not share a first language. It is therefore advisable to follow up the telephone conversation with a clear written statement of what has been agreed. A short e-mail message confirming the content of the discussion, like the one in Box 10.1, can prevent misunderstandings and future problems.

Box 10.1: A client's e-mail to confirm the content of a telephone conversation

To: ......

From: ....

Date: ......

I am writing with reference to (conversation and date). *On behalf of* (organisation), *I am pleased that you are able to work with us on* (project or initiative). *We agreed that you will prepare and lead a workshop on the results of the evaluation and help the staff to develop plans for the future of the programme. The work is expected to cover four days: one for preparation, two for running the workshop, and one for developing a report.* (Organisation) *will pay you the sum of X and cover your travel and subsistence costs. You will provide a short written report on the process of the workshop; but the content will be recorded and turned into a report by* (organisation) *staff.*

If the consultant does not receive confirmation of a telephone agreement within a day of the phone call, he or she should send an e-mail to the client, confirming his or her understanding of the agreement, as in Box 10.2.

Box 10.2: A consultant's e-mail to confirm the content of a telephone conversation

To: ......

From: ....

Date: ......

I am writing with reference to (conversation and date). *I look forward to working with you on* (project or initiative). *We agreed that I will prepare and lead a workshop on the results of the evaluation and help the staff of your organisation to develop plans for the future of the programme. The work is expected to cover four days: one for preparation, two for running the workshop, and one for developing a report. You will pay me the sum of X and cover my travel and subsistence costs. I will provide a short written report on the process of the workshop; but the content will be recorded and turned into a report by your staff.*

Under pressure to get an assignment started, both parties may make verbal agreements; the work may be done well; and both parties may be clear about what is required. But if things go wrong, there are no reliable records of what was agreed about the work to be done, the methodology, the fees, the scope and style of the consultancy, and other vital matters.

Suppose that the consultant starts work on the basis of a verbal agreement, but then the consultancy cannot be completed or properly carried out. Is the client liable for paying the consultant for the time spent on the assignment? The answer may be that the client is liable if the consultant was working on the best information available and can demonstrate that he or she had actually started the work. The client may not be liable if the consultant knew that the verbal agreement was to be replaced by a written agreement. If the client has agreed to draft or send a written contract, or suggested a meeting to sign a contract, then the consultant knows that the detailed agreement will be in the written version, and anything that he or she does before seeing that contract will be done at his or her own risk. For this reason, consultants are often understandably unwilling to start work until they have the written contract in their hands.

However, the client in this case might be liable to reimburse the consultant for preparation time spent on work which was clearly necessary for the success of the assignment, even if the consultant knew that a written contract was going to be produced which would define the terms of the agreement precisely. For example, the consultant might begin to obtain a visa to travel to the assignment. Any reasonable person would agree that such an action was a necessary preparation for the task, and that the consultant's expenses should be reimbursed, even if the consultancy did not proceed.

Good sense will generally mean that this sort of situation is resolved amicably. However, it is important to be aware of the risks of allowing work to start without a clear written contract.

Performance contracts

A contract can also result from the actions of the client and the consultant. If a consultant performs work for a client without any written or oral agreement, there is still a legally binding contract whereby the client must pay for the work done. This applies to the following instances:

- **Extensions to an assignment:** a client may ask a consultant to do additional work after the end of the assignment, without extending the formal contract or providing a new ToR.

- **Variations to an assignment:** changes may be made while the work is on-going, if it is found that some aspects are not necessary, or that time should be spent on another aspect.

To avoid potential problems, it is always best to agree such changes in writing and append the terms to the original agreements.

Types of contract

Several common types of contract reflect the different ways in which consultants may be paid:

- A **contract for a specific one-off piece of work**, as defined in a Terms of Reference.

- A **call-down contract**, established when a client is likely to have a continuing need for consultancy support, but it is difficult to predict the exact nature of that support. In such cases the client may pre-select a consultant or a company to provide the support, as and when needed, for a fee that is agreed in advance. The client should establish which particular consultant(s) will be providing the services, and should also establish a financial limit for the period in question. Once this is exceeded, the contract should be re-negotiated as needed. It is common for large agencies to establish such contracts with consultancy firms, to provide back-up support for particular programmes over a number of years.

- A **retainer contract**, appropriate when the consultant is providing regular advice or support to the client, such as advice on legal matters. For example, the contract defines what is to be provided, and the time available per month over the course of a year. Because such contracts provide a regular income over a period longer than normal, it is usual to agree a reduced daily rate. Such arrangements need to be monitored closely.

Confidentiality, copyright, and intellectual property

The legal ownership of information and knowledge is a major issue in consultancy work. The nature of the work means that a consultant may be admitted into the heart of an organisation and entrusted with a wide range of sensitive information. The information may be financial (rates of pay or costs, for example) or moral (relating, for instance, to a confidential disciplinary case). Even apparently trivial knowledge such as relations between members of a team may become highly sensitive. The responsible consultant will automatically maintain confidentiality and work in the best interests of the client at all times.

To protect client agencies, most contracts include a clause committing the consultant to treat information acquired during the consultancy as confidential. Often the clause provides for the consultant's future use of information arising from the assignment, on the condition that prior written permission is obtained. Such clauses may be a cause for concern: partly because there is some uncertainty about what actually is confidential information, and also because these clauses may impede the sharing of learning from consultancy work.

Note that information provided to a consultant during the assignment may be considered as confidential by an informant, but it may not actually be so. If the information is already in the public domain (that is to say, it is widely known or could be easily obtained), then the consultant can use it if necessary in his or her own work. Similarly, information that the consultant possessed before the assignment is not covered by a confidentiality clause, even if the same information is passed to the consultant as if it were confidential.

Consultants need to protect themselves against the risk of abusing the trust put in them by staff or other informants during the course of an assignment. It is good practice to explain to all informants how information that they provide will be used, allowing them to choose whether or not to take part in the interview. In certain circumstances it may be appropriate to assure informants that their identity will be protected, and their views will be reported anonymously.

Difficulties may arise when a consultant wants to share learning from a piece of work with a third party, in the form of a copy of the final report. However, the report belongs to the client, and the consultant should ask the client to send a copy directly to the person concerned, or to give the consultant written permission to send a copy.

The issue of intellectual property should be covered by the terms and conditions of the contract. If a consultant is asked to research and develop something specific for a client, such as a strategy for working in a particular country, a training module for staff, or a computer system, the client commonly owns the intellectual property that results. If the consultant uses a model or system, such as a training module, that he or she has developed prior to starting the work in question, then the consultant retains ownership.

It may be more difficult to identify ownership of material that is generally available or partly in the public domain. Training material is a good example, in that trainees clearly gain access to certain information and ideas and can take away the handouts and their own notes. However, the consultant trainer may not want the client organisation to use the material to run training courses of its own. It can be hard for the consultant to demonstrate that the training material was unique or wholly his or her own product. This is especially the case where the training is not accredited. Nevertheless, the consultant can insist that the training material is not used for further training events, and in such a case a clause would be added to the contract, or an additional written agreement would be made: effectively a second contract. This must be discussed during the negotiations before the contract is signed. The consultant needs to be clear what he or she is seeking to protect. A large organisation may require the same training course to be run in a range of different offices, so there may be the possibility of several follow-up contracts; but a small agency may not require more than a single training event, so it may not be necessary to protect the material from future use.

Failure to deliver

A surprising number of clients in our small survey claimed that they had not paid consultants because the latter had not delivered a satisfactory piece of work. Commonly a contract will stipulate that a final payment will be made on delivery of a final product (usually a written report) of 'satisfactory' quality. If the final product is deemed not to be satisfactory, then the final payment may be withheld (or paid grudgingly, in order to avoid unpleasant conflict), and the matter ends there. This is an extremely inadequate response to poor work, and it brings the practice of consultancy into disrepute. Consultants seem to be as concerned about this problem as clients are, because bad consultants can give consultancy a bad reputation.

When a consultancy has not worked out well, there are several steps that should be taken. It is necessary to examine what went wrong, and why. Consultancies sometimes fail despite the best efforts of all parties. A feedback and evaluation session is very important for all consultancies, no matter how short. Too often this aspect is ignored, and time is not set aside to ensure that feedback is done well. For example, the final exchange is the delivery of a report, or a reporting meeting which ends shortly before the consultants return to their home locations.

The failure to conduct a proper feedback session means that the client has to assess the usefulness of the final product (which might be a trained group of staff or partners, for example, but is most commonly a report) and decide whether it meets the organisation's criteria without further input from the consultant. The consultant may be many miles away by this time and is left wondering how the work has been received.

When a client feels that the work has not met the specifications, the manager should immediately contact the consultant and try to reach a satisfactory solution. First, both sides should try to renegotiate the outcomes. Second, the consultant should be given the opportunity to make good the contract. Most consultants want to provide a good service and will offer to do whatever further work needs to be done, normally at no extra cost. Third, both sides could develop a new short contract to cover what is now needed from the piece of work.

As we have already noted, contracts should set out the mechanisms for settling disputes if initial informal attempts fail to bring a satisfactory conclusion. Contracts should also describe how a contract can be ended if either side defaults on the agreement.

Cancellation clauses

Contracts should incorporate cancellation clauses to specify the consequences if either the client or the consultant is unable to go forward with the consultancy once the contract has been signed.

Late cancellation of work by the client is a constant problem faced by consultants. One way to reduce the impact of this is for the parties to agree on a cancellation clause, stating that if the client cancels the work, the consultant is entitled to a proportion of the fees that would have been paid if the work had gone ahead. The clause may contain a sliding scale, so that a cancellation notified within a stipulated period would involve a payment of a small proportion of the fees, whereas a very late cancellation would incur payment of all or almost all of the fees. (See Annex 3 for further discussion of this point.)

The rationale for this is explained by the way in which consultants allocate time for contracts. If a consultant is fairly sure that a piece of work will start in a month's time, he or she will tend not to take offers of work relating to the period immediately before or after the agreed dates. This is done partly to allow for possible changes, but mostly in order to protect the consultant from excessive commitments. If the agreement is then cancelled, the consultant will have lost not only that particular earning opportunity, but also the opportunity of other potential assignments.

Liability for health and safety

Responsible clients should be concerned about their duty of care for the health and safety of any consultants working for them, equal to that provided to their staff. Conversely, the terms and conditions of contracts will often stipulate that a consultant should take all reasonable measures to comply with the health-and-safety regulations of the organisation and will avoid doing anything that puts others at risk. Depending on the nature of the assignment, a client may make the issuing of a contract dependent on medical clearance. Clients may need to take particular precautions when sending consultants to politically unstable areas and conflict zones, requiring consultants to agree to abide by the agency's security procedures.

While the client has certain responsibilities towards the consultant, consultants have a responsibility to inform themselves of the situation into which they will be going. The general rule for consultants is that they should not take undue risks and should not agree to do anything about which they feel unduly uncomfortable.

Insurance

When we asked consultants what insurance they expected clients to provide, we received a very wide range of responses. Things are in a state of flux. One uncertainty arises when consultants work for organisations by whom they were previously employed as members of staff: they may not understand that they will not be protected by the same cover that is provided for regular staff.

Clients should review their organisation's obligations and liabilities with regard to the local situation under consideration, including national laws and tax regimes, and act accordingly, checking whether individual consultants are appropriately insured for the assignment in question. In most cases this means that clients should check that consultants are adequately protected by their own personal insurance policies, and they should draw attention to clauses in contracts which stipulate that the client does not have liability. In future it may be necessary to insist that consultants sign a statement to affirm that they are adequately protected, and that they indemnify the client from claims. This could constitute a clause in the contract.

Consultants need to ensure that they are adequately covered for sickness, accidents, loss of property, and public liability. They should study their policies to check that their type of work is appropriately covered. Premiums can usually be claimed as a business expense when calculating tax bills.

For work in areas considered to pose particular risks (because of prevailing armed conflict, for example), client organisations should consider reimbursing the supplement that consultants will have to pay to their insurers. They should also consider putting the consultant in contact with specialist underwriters.

Accidents and ill health

Insurance against accidents and ill health should cover the costs of treatment in the countries where the consultant will work, and also the costs of being repatriated to his or her home country. Most travel-insurance policies will provide this kind of cover, but there is a big difference between policies that include the actual provision of air-ambulance services and those that only reimburse costs incurred. The consultant may be left having to pay for the medical care in the first instance. In practice, most client organisations will accept that they have a responsibility to help consultants to obtain any necessary medical attention.

Loss of property

Consultants should insure their possessions and money when they are on assignment and ensure that essential equipment – such as a laptop or digital camera – is covered by the policy. Such equipment may have to be insured under special policies over and above normal travel-insurance or household policies; this can be considered a legitimate part of normal business expenses.

Travel-insurance policies are notorious for having low limits on the value of each item that is lost, and a low total limit allowed per claim. The limits do not normally allow a consultant to recover the costs of the high-value items mentioned above. In addition, some policies deduct an excess payment (the part of the loss that has to be covered by the person who is insured) for each item that is claimed, rather than applying it to the whole claim.

Public liability

Consultants should consider whether or not they need to be protected by public-liability insurance. This might help if someone were hurt during a piece of work that the consultant was involved in: for example, if a participant at a workshop fell over some of the consultant's equipment and was hurt. The chance of such an accident occurring may be small, and the probability that the person who was hurt would seek compensation from the consultant (and not from the client organisation or the owner of the venue) may be low; but consultants should be aware of this risk.

In some situations, consultancy firms will have negotiated public-liability and professional-indemnity insurance (see below) to cover freelance consultants who are carrying out work for them.

Professional indemnity

Non-specialist consultants who work only within the international development sector are usually not covered by professional-indemnity insurance (PII). Firstly, it can be expensive to obtain; secondly, the risk of being sued for professional failings is extremely low. PII provides cover in cases where a consultant's advice or input is found to be inaccurate and causes problems or losses to the client. Consultants who provide financial or legal advice need this kind of insurance; but it does not protect them from claims for damages arising from misconduct or misrepresentation of their competencies. Consultants who work in the UK voluntary sector may find that they need PII in order to work in situations where they are in contact with vulnerable people, or visiting their homes. Proof of cover may be a condition attached to the award of a contract. A client hiring a consultant to provide legal or financial advice should check to see whether the consultant has appropriate PII insurance.

A consultant could be at risk if he or she causes damage to property belonging to the client agency; but the risk may be greater if damage is caused to property belonging to another company or person. This might be something very slight, like marking the walls of a room when posting up flipcharts; but it could be more serious, like spilling ink or coffee on a pale carpet. The costs of repairing this kind of damage could be very high, and the consultant should assess the possibility of being faced with bills for such repair work.

At present it may be acceptable to work in the sector without insurance protection, but it seems increasingly likely that cover will become essential, if the current tendency to invoke the law to obtain compensation for minor accidents and inconvenience continues. It would require only a few cases of a consultant being sued for marking the walls of a hotel for clients to insist that all consultants have adequate insurance cover. Trends like these are discussed in greater detail in Chapter 15.

Guarantee of consultancy work

Some consultants offer a guarantee that they will provide a satisfactory service and will make good any unsatisfactory outcome. The guarantee would be presented with the CV during the initial contact with the client. It implies that the consultant takes his or her work seriously. A guarantee is somewhat similar to a statement of values or a code of conduct, in that it has to be implemented by the author. It is doubtful that the guarantee would be called upon in a legal dispute, and it may not in itself make the consultant more attractive to a potential client. The main value of a guarantee may be that it draws the attention of both sides to the question of quality and the need to review the work when it has been completed.

The contents of a standard contract

The content of most consultancy work is defined by the Terms of Reference, so a contract has only to set out the general legal agreement between the client and the consultant on which the work described in the ToR will be done. The ToR may be modified during a consultancy, but the contract may not need to be altered, even if some of the content of the work is altered.

In Annex 1 we quote some typical clauses that commonly appear in contracts.[14] Here we will simply describe some of the types of clause that would normally be included in a consultancy contract in the international development sector.

Many contracts are very simple documents, covering no more than the specific conditions under which the work will be done. However, even relatively short contracts now include a range of other clauses that make the legal situation clearer. Once a standard contract has been developed, a template can be produced for use in a wide range of work. It will contain general sections that remain largely unchanged, and shorter specific sections (such as name of consultant, details of timing, etc.) that can be easily adjusted for each consultancy.

A full contract will typically contain the following sections.

Definitions and description

- The title of the consultancy.
- A brief description of the work, with reference to the Terms of Reference.
- A definition of the respective parties to the contract, so that the generic terms 'client' and 'consultant' can be used in other clauses.

Payments

- Fees: total sums to be paid, and daily rate if applicable.
- Reimbursable expenses: what is covered, and how claims should be made.
- Payment schedule: the dates by which sums will be paid.
- Currency and method of payment: cheque, bank transfer, or cash.
- Instructions for the presentation of invoices and other documentation required for audit purposes: time sheets, receipts, and ticket stubs, etc.

Conditions for starting and stopping

- Start-dates for contract and operational work.
- End-dates for contract and for work.
- How alterations or modifications can be made.
- How the client could terminate the contract.
- How the consultant could terminate the contract.
- Compensation due if the contract were terminated prematurely by either party.
- What to do if the project has to be cancelled due to circumstances beyond the control of either party *(force majeure)*.
- How disputes should be managed.
- The legal system under which any conflict would be resolved.

Duties of the consultant

- Standards of behaviour and discipline: to work to the highest possible standards, to inform the client of difficulties, to deliver original material, avoid abusing intellectual property or defaming the client in any way, etc.
- Conflict of interest: to declare any potential conflict of interest arising from assignments for other clients.
- Confidentiality: not to exploit information obtained during the consultancy.
- Sub-contracting: not to involve other people in the work, or in parts of it, without the agreement of the client.
- Reporting: to submit a report according to the stated requirements.
- Tax: to be responsible for paying his or her own tax.
- Insurance and liabilities: to be responsible for obtaining insurance against specified risks, as agreed with the client.
- Reputation of the client: to consult the client before making public reference to the work covered by the assignment.
- Property of the client: to take reasonable care of documents and equipment provided by the client, and to return them as agreed.
- Follow-on work: to refer to the client any offer of further work arising from this assignment for a defined period of time after completion of the contract.

Duties of the client

- Facilities: to make available to the consultant certain specified facilities and services.
- Support: to provide specified support (in such matters as obtaining permits or visas and providing introductions).
- Data protection: how the client may use information relating to the consultant.

In Annex 1, each of these sections is illustrated by sample clauses[15] that can be adapted for particular purposes.

Clients who are issuing contracts for the first time would be advised to take professional legal advice, either from an independent company or from their in-house legal adviser, if their organisation employs one.

11 | Managing a consultancy: from preparation to feedback

This chapter considers management issues for both clients and consultants during the preparatory phases, the core work, and the final stages of the consultancy. It concludes by considering the special cases of participatory work and capacity strengthening.

Managing the preparation and start-up

The manager who initiates the consultancy has the following responsibilities during this phase:

- confirm who will manage the whole process
- inform all those who may be involved in or affected by the consultancy
- agree the roles and general responsibilities of the team members
- agree schedules and lines of communication
- provide consultants with background material and briefings
- arrange all necessary travel, accommodation, and subsistence
- assess risks to health, safety, and security.

Identifying the consultancy manager and informing stakeholders

One person should be confirmed as the manager of the consultancy, and this person should act as the first point of contact. If the consultancy affects a large number of people or departments within the client organisation, or several organisations working together, it may be helpful to set up a steering committee so that they can follow progress and make comments on the consultancy as it develops.

Consultancies sometimes fail simply because interested parties are not properly informed in advance. The client should make sure that all stake-holders are appropriately involved and kept informed; this will increase the likelihood that they will be committed to supporting the consultancy.

'I was stuck in (capital city) for about ten days, trying to get a travel permit. Finally I made the journey to (town), to find that the project manager was not expecting me and was planning to leave the next day. We were not able to discuss the work at all, and later he savaged my report for not being well informed.'
(A consultant)

Agreeing roles and responsibilities

Defining the roles and responsibilities of both client and consultant in the management of the contract is key to the success of the consultancy. Consultants should be told as soon as possible the names of the people with whom they will be working, and the names of the people to whom they should report.

A consultant working as a team leader needs to know how the other members of the team are being recruited, and how they will be managed. Some consultants will refuse to accept a leadership role if they have no influence over the selection of team members. If the consultant is to be the team leader, before the main work begins he or she should ideally contact other members of the team in order to establish roles and responsibilities. The building of relationships between the members of a team, who may be brought together specifically for the assignment, is as important as the building of relationships between the consultant and the client.

A team may work together better and learn more from each other and from the work if they plan to review their work together at regular, perhaps daily, intervals. A sequence of feedback and round-up meetings allows the consultants to monitor their own learning as the consultancy progresses, and makes them better able to report to the client as well.

'On the first consultancy I met the team members on a Monday afternoon, and we had to start work on the Tuesday. We had hardly enough time to decide on the methods before we split up again. We recommended that in the next phase there should be more time for team building. They circulated everyone's CV and they gave us a whole day to get to know each other and discuss the work in a more relaxed way, which was great. When we got down to the urgent stuff the next day, it all went much more smoothly.'
(A consultant)

Schedules and lines of communication

It is vital to agree a timetable of work, and to adhere to it. However, timing is often the most contentious and difficult issue in the management of consultancies. The client should set out a realistic schedule, based on reasonable norms for the various stages of work. Consultants often feel that they are put under artificial time pressures, but this can be avoided by explaining the organisational constraints to the consultant. Clients should also consider what measures can be taken if the consultancy does not run according to their ideal timetable.

As well as a timetable, the consultant and client should agree on a mechanism for reporting. A protocol for e-mail communication should be agreed, with fall-back arrangements in case e-mail connections cannot be made.

Preparation of background material and briefing of consultants

Once the contract has been confirmed, consultants will be keen to have access to background material. Essential briefing materials – including an inventory of information sources – should be clearly identified during the early planning stages, and it is the manager's responsibility to ensure that these are prepared in good time.

The most relevant documents should be gathered together for convenience, and some of the key documents should be copied so that consultants have immediate access to them. Staff resources permitting, it is useful to make one person responsible for helping consultants to locate information. Electronic versions of key documents are often the most useful format, for easy sharing and for reference while travelling.

Briefing consultants is an important element of the preparation process. It should aim to achieve all the following ends.

- Provide basic information about the client organisation.
- Explain the background and origin of the consultancy and describe preparatory work, including the involvement of staff and other stakeholders (for example, who have commented on the ToR).
- Identify factors that could impede progress.
- Identify any training required by the consultants (for example, familiarisation with the client's information systems), and arrange for it to be provided before the core work begins.

Consultants may be in a difficult position if they are not aware of tensions between the interested parties, or if they are not told who has been consulted and who has not. Consultants should ask for names of others who should be interviewed, in order to collect the widest possible range of views. New ideas will always emerge as work progresses, so consultants should not accept a schedule of pre-arranged meetings which allows no flexibility to interview newly identified contacts, to hold unforeseen meetings, or to arrange extra site visits.

Logistics

It is vital that arrangements for travel, accommodation, and working space are well organised, in order to ensure the smooth running and effective use of consultancy inputs. The contract should stipulate who is responsible for these arrangements. Where the consultant is responsible for organising logistics (such as buying tickets for air travel), time should be allowed for this between the award of the contract and the start of the work. The consultant may not be able to invest time in organising work until a confirmed contract has been received (and indeed he or she would be unwise to do so).

Poorly organised logistics signal that the consultancy is poorly conceived or poorly supported by parts of the organisation. If prior arrangements are inadequate, particularly if the consultant is to visit areas where access to programme sites is difficult, valuable time will be wasted.

Health, safety, and security

The consultancy manager should ensure that risks to health, safety, and security have been fully assessed and that the consultant has been made fully aware of them. It is important to inform consultants of any agency policies and procedures that are non-negotiable and constitute part of the client organisation's duty of care to its staff and visitors. Examples might be the wearing of safety belts in the organisation's vehicles, and adhering to certain security protocols. Consultants unfamiliar with the areas that they are to visit will welcome information on matters such as dress code and relevant health precautions.

The client will have to take responsibility if the consultant is taken ill. The client has a duty of care to the consultant, as to other staff, and the duty is moral as well as legal. Nevertheless, the client should ask the consultant to confirm that he or she is in good health at the start of the assignment, and that his or her private insurance cover is adequate and appropriate. (See Chapter 10 for more comments on this point.)

The client and consultant should discuss the security situation and potential difficulties that might cause a consultancy to be abandoned. The client can insist that the consultant follows the organisation's security guidelines, and the consultant has the right to avoid putting himself or herself at risk. Where necessary, updates on the security situation should be part of routine communication between the client and consultants. Both sides need to agree on communication methods and schedules, and fall-back arrangements if communications fail. Obviously the major concerns are for the personal safety of all those involved, and there should be clearly identified strategies for reducing risks and a mechanism for abandoning the work if appropriate.

Managing the core work of the consultancy

In principle, the division of roles and responsibilities and the reporting systems between the client and the consultant will be spelled out in the contract/ToR and discussed during the briefing. The manager is responsible for the following:

- actively managing the relationship with the consultant
- supporting management within the consultancy team
- supporting access to informants (for example, by providing translation services)
- monitoring the quality of work through feedback and reporting
- amending the assignment requirements where necessary, while trying to keep the consultancy within the terms of its agreed scope and budget.

Building the consultant–client relationship

The relationship between the client/manager and the consultant is crucial to the success of the consultancy. Both sides need to invest in building trust and establishing an honest exchange of ideas and information. This should be seen as separate from the work of briefing or actually starting work on the consultancy, even though all these things are going on at the same time. The client/manager and the consultant will be assessing each other's personal qualities, as well as their professional skills. The client–consultant relationship may be subject to power dynamics of gender, culture, and social background, and both parties need to pay attention to these considerations.

During this stage an unofficial briefing on organisational culture may take place. A good consultant will pay special attention to any indications of internal tensions and difficulties that were not part of the official briefing.

Successful consultancy work is largely dependent on whether or not the consultant can talk to the right people. The client should have timed the consultancy so that all the key people are available when needed and are putting time aside to make themselves genuinely available.

'I called and called, and he was never available. Then we arranged to meet, but he cancelled at the last minute. Finally, I decided just to drop in while I was in the building talking to someone else. I found him in, and we talked for over an hour, although I had no appointment. I began to understand why his time management meant that he had never been available to meet me.'
(A consultant)

It is not uncommon for consultants to find that they have a meeting scheduled with someone who seems to have no knowledge that could be useful to the consultancy. Usually this is the result of the manager's efforts to be inclusive. It does not seem polite in such circumstances to abandon an interview as soon as the mismatch is discovered. In fact, meetings that initially appear to be inappropriate to the consultancy can sometimes yield learning for one or other party, or identify relevant key contacts.

Sometimes it is appropriate to allow the team to start working and then schedule a review meeting to adjust the proposed work in the light of conditions 'on the ground'. This may be formalised as an 'inception meeting', and in some cases the consultant will have to produce an inception report.

Team building and management lines

Consultancies often require teams of consultants with a range of skills and experience. Although it is increasingly common for consultants to be contracted from the country or region where the work is taking place, it is still common for clients to build teams that consist of both local and international consultants.

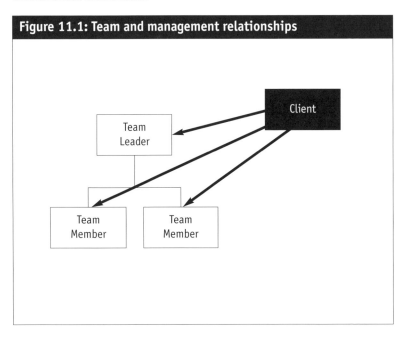

Figure 11.1: Team and management relationships

Figure 11.1 shows the strong contractual relationships that normally exist between consultants and the client, and the relatively weak relationships that exist between the team leader and the other members of the team. The team leader is frequently given a very short time in which to develop these weak relationships into something that will be strong enough to cope with working within a tight timetable.

The team leader should assign roles according to the particular abilities of the team members. The client should check with the team leader that he or she has done this and is making the most of the strengths of the individual members. As with the client–consultant relationship, relationships between team members are subject to a wide range of power dynamics. Gender, age, ethnicity, and educational background may all influence the way in which the team members work together. The team leader should pay attention to these dynamics and intervene where necessary in order to get the best performance out of each member of the team.

Experienced consultants, when asked to lead a team, will often insist on having a clear contractual hold over the other team members, and without it they may not accept the assignment. The team leader may be better able to manage the team if individual consultants' contracts state that they will not be paid until the team leader is satisfied with their contributions. Some organisations require the team leader to sign a form to confirm the acceptability of a team member's work before payment is issued. A problem arises for the client when the team members request their fees, claiming that they have fulfilled their obligations, when the team leader has still to deliver the report upon which all fee payments depend.

Another problem that agencies based in the North frequently mention is the difficulty of obtaining acceptable reports from national consultants, who may not be writing in their first language, or may be unfamiliar with the style of reporting required by the client or the donor. Rather than address the underlying reasons for this, clients put together teams containing both local and international consultants, in the hope that the international consultants will take responsibility for compiling and submitting the reports on time.

> 'We were contracted as two equal solo consultants, each with specific expertise. While we were expected to work together as equals, I was asked to review the report of the national consultant in order for him to receive payment. I felt this put me in an invidious position, but the client would not see it. In the event, my fellow consultant had tremendous difficulty in producing a written document. The local office of the donor paid him, and I was expected to complete the work, using his material. In future I would not accept such a situation.'
> (An international consultant)

Some clients assume that people will simply work together well, without clear lines of command or an established method for solving problems when they arise. Management lines should be kept clear and simple, and the client needs to be very supportive of the team leader in order to get the best out of everyone in the team.

Differences in contracts can make it harder to work as a team. Differences in fee rates paid to (or demanded by) local and international consultants reflect the differences that exist between the salaries of people working in different countries. However, these differences need not be aggravated by the methods chosen for payment: for example, by paying actuals to international consultants and *per diem* expenses to local consultants, thus making it difficult for them to stay in the same hotel. Clients should provide the same working conditions for local and international consultants. Team building and efficient working are helped if team members stay in the same place for the duration of the work. Paying actual costs for hotels and a small non-accountable *per diem* seems a reasonable means of ensuring that local and international consultants are best able to work together. But a non-accountable *per diem* to cover lodging and ancillary expenses may encourage some consultants to seek cheaper accommodation in order to save money, which means that the team becomes dispersed and team work becomes more difficult. Staying in the same place can be made a condition of the contract, even if a consultant lives in the city where the work is taking place.

Translation and interpreters

Translation is a key consideration in many consultancies. Interpreters are often necessary when key informants need to be interviewed in their first language. Finding good translators requires experience and judgement, and it may not be possible for the consultant to do this within the typically short period of a consultancy.

Interpretation is a skilled task. In most cases the interpreter and the interviewer need to work together for some time, in order to develop an easy style of collaboration. If interpreters will be used, extra time should be allowed for each interview and also for testing and practising the questions to be asked.

> 'Translation is a bit like participation – everyone wants you to be able to talk to communities, but clients often forget to include a budget line for it. Even if you have the funds, it can be hard to find a translator who is also independent of the process. I have often had to resort to asking staff members to do it – with the increased pressure on them and the loss of independence that this entails.'
> (A consultant)

Clients and consultants should be aware of the imbalance of power that often prevails when consultants are interviewing partners and programme beneficiaries. The people who are least powerful may be excluded because they cannot speak to the consultants. Women, if they tend not to venture beyond their own household or community, often speak fewer languages than men and may need help with translation; they may also prefer to speak to a female interpreter. The client should plan for the additional costs and additional time involved in this type of exercise. The consultant should ensure that the client is aware of this and, if there is a lack of finance and time, should prepare the client for the fact that less is likely to be achieved than was originally hoped for.

Feedback on progress: no surprises

In a good consultancy, both the client and the consultant are aware of findings and analysis as they develop, so that the feedback contains no surprises. A good consultant will work hard to keep the client informed, especially if bad news seems probable. Bad news should not come as a surprise, since the client may find it difficult to accept it easily and may be forced to react without having adequate time to consider all the information. The client who has had time to think about results as they emerge will be much better equipped to respond to the recommendations of a consultancy.

A common complaint made by consultants is that the key client or manager is not available when important decisions need to be made. If it is difficult for the manager to be available all the time, an agreement to contact one another at predetermined times is the best compromise. Sometimes an inexperienced consultant may feel reluctant to contact a client about problems, for fear of appearing weak or incompetent. A fixed schedule helps to resolve this problem.

An effective means of checking on performance is to ask for written material at key stages of the consultancy. It can be difficult to assess achievement on the basis of verbal reports. Some consultants talk extremely well about the work that they are doing, but later they deliver poor written material. A very short written report should be enough to demonstrate the true potential of the on-going work. It needs to involve only a summary of key findings in bullet-point format, so that the work of writing does not feel like an additional burden.

Interim reports and feedback meetings

Often the timescale of a consultancy makes it impossible to produce the full report while a consultant is in-country or still in direct contact with the client or other stakeholders. The production of a very short interim report (or *aide memoire*), setting out the main findings, can be a valuable step in promoting exchanges between the consultant, the client, and other stakeholders.

Such a document does not need to be longer than one or two pages, provided that it summarises the main findings and indicates any contentious issues that warrant discussion. This gives stakeholders the opportunity to assist in the analysis and to give their first reactions to the findings. Some skill is required in presenting contentious or negative findings. In evaluation work in particular, consultants need to take great care when wording their observations if their findings reflect negatively on the client organisation. The *aide memoire* allows consultants to present their findings as provisional, and to verify their analysis with those involved.

Interim feedback meetings allow wide-ranging discussions that may play an essential part in improving the final report. They also make it more likely that there will be a concerted institutional reaction to the consultancy, rather than disappointingly dispersed reactions to a written report.

Amending the contract

It is common to have to modify work as a consultancy progresses. In most cases the changes required will be small. The contract can remain the same, and the ToR can be amended fairly easily. However, sometimes a major change is necessary, and this necessitates a clearly stated adjustment.

Sometimes clients ask a consultant to do a bit more work at the end of a consultancy. This may seem justified because the work has genuinely grown, and the consultant is fully briefed and in a good position to carry it out. It is an attractive option if the manager does not need to raise a new contract but simply extend the existing one. The process of adding to a consultancy is sometimes called 'contract creep'.

Contract creep is not necessarily a bad thing. However, it becomes negative and damaging where there is no good record of the process, and where better options are ignored because it is simply easier to give extra work to someone who is already on contract. Contract creep can result in the unauthorised and unrecorded use of funds, putting clients in an uncomfortable situation and leading to consultants doing work with no agreed contract to fall back on.

By far the most common change to an agreement is to limit the extent of the work in order to focus on fewer aspects than are defined in the ToR – either because the ToR were over-ambitious, or because the work has taken longer than expected. The scope of a consultancy might be reduced in terms of activities or of geographical coverage. For example:

- *We can assess the water and health service work but not the credit component.*
- *We can look at the project work in two villages, but not all four.*
- *We can examine the impact on health, but not do a full cost–benefit analysis.*

It is easy to assume that everyone will remember that some of the work has been dropped, but this is a mistake. Reducing the scope of the assignment is the most common cause of disagreements at the end of a consultancy, when one party believes that some aspect of the work should have been covered, but the other believes that it was agreed to leave it out.

When any change is made to the original contract or ToR, both the client and the consultant should be very clear about what has been added or excluded during the re-negotiation, to avoid any possibility of confusion at the end of the contract. It is very important for the client to keep a written record of the decisions made, as and when they happen, and the rationale for the decisions as understood at the time. Any change of scope or focus should also be documented.

It is particularly important to record any changes in the use of budgets and resources. This makes it possible to construct what is called an 'audit trail'. Anyone who was not present at the time should be able to follow the chain of decisions and understand what happened, and why. At the very least, the change should be recorded in an e-mail message confirming the content of meetings at which decisions were made.

Consultants should be wary of changes in reporting relations or changes in staff roles once a consultancy has started. They should be concerned if new people or staff with lower authority are introduced at a later stage, and should insist on a consistent allocation of appropriate staff to the consultancy. Consultants should not start a new piece of work without considering whether they should also start a new contract for it. In some circumstances, it may be necessary to suspend the work in order to review the situation more carefully.

Managing the end of a consultancy: finalisation and follow-up

This phase consists of the following elements:
- managing the writing of the final report
- giving feedback to consultants
- approving the work done and closing the contract
- taking forward any recommendations
- assessing the consultancy with the consultants
- evaluating the effects of the consultancy work
- coping with apparent failure.

The final report

The final product of most consultancies is a written document. Generally it is the responsibility of the team leader to compile a report based on input from other team members. It should be noted that good field workers are not always good writers. Clients should consider providing extra help with writing or editing, or allowing reports to be presented in local languages and then translated as necessary at the agency's expense. (There may in any case be a need for a report written in the local language, for the benefit of local stakeholders.)

Experience suggests that reports should be written, or at least drafted, before the team disperses at the end of a consultancy. The ToR should specify that the writing must be done while the team is in the same place, normally the country where the work is being done. Adequate time should be allowed for this in the contract: it is very common for both clients and consultants to underestimate the amount of time that will be required for the actual writing.

Once the team has split up, especially if people are in different countries, with new priorities, there is very little that can be done to ensure that a report is produced. Even the threat of not being paid may not be enough to get someone who is now deeply involved in new work and other demands to address the difficulties of writing a late report.

See Chapter 6 for further guidance on the commissioning and writing of reports.

Delivery on time

One thing that clients like is short reports; and another is short reports that are delivered on time. The timing of a consultancy report is often linked to an internal decision-making process, and a delay may be very inconvenient for the client.

However, meeting deadlines is often a major problem. Part of the reason for this is a failure to calculate just how long it really takes to write a report. Inexperienced clients often insist on impossibly tight deadlines. Inexperienced consultants may fail to meet deadlines, but even experienced ones sometimes make over-optimistic assessments of how much time they will need. Consultants may feel that it is better to accept the deadline even if it appears very tight, rather than risk losing the job.

Most consultants in our survey said that writing always takes longer than planned, but they always feel under pressure to accept a shorter period of time. This means that clients will continue to expect them to do so. Some norm should be accepted: for example, that it will take five full consultant days to produce a 25-page report with 50 pages of annexes, to an acceptable standard that will not require a great deal of editorial work.

Writing the report is a critical phase of the work, and adequate time must be allowed for it.

Making, and justifying, recommendations

A responsible consultant will produce a prioritised list of recommendations on which the client can act. It may be appropriate to set out 'ideal' recommendations, but also to submit less ambitious recommendations that take account of the reality of the situation. The recommendations should relate to the ability of the client and other relevant stakeholders to act, and must refer back to the ToR and the original reasons for the consultancy.

The client and other interested parties will want to see the evidence that the consultant used in arriving at a judgement. The consultant must ensure that the steps in the recommended process are clear, so that there can be discussion of each one, independently of the others. Overlap between the different steps will make it much harder to work out how to proceed. This level of analysis is very important, especially if the recommendations are contentious in any way.

For example, a consultant producing a report on health care in a particular community may examine a health centre's records and interview the nurse in charge. Drawing on these observations, the consultant may judge that levels of disease are very high, compared with similar situations elsewhere, and that more could be done to address the issue. He or she will then recommend the particular steps that should be taken. However, the consultant's observations, judgement, and recommendations are all open to challenge. For example, the health centre's records may not be accurate, or the nurse may not be a reliable witness. The consultant's judgement of the situation may over-estimate the seriousness of the problem. Even if the consultant's judgement is accurate, the recommendations may be unrealistic. Even if the recommendations are good, it may be that the client organisation does not have the skills or resources to implement them, or it may have more urgent priorities. Consultant and client may disagree at several different points in the process, so the consultant's reasoning must be made as clear as possible.

Management response to recommendations

Some organisations attach the management's response to the consultancy report, thus creating a double document. In this way the reactions to the various stages of the consultancy can be assessed, and the responses can be judged against the recommendations contained in the report. The responses could be to accept, or modify, or reject the findings or the recommendations. The development of a double document does not imply that the management agrees with the consultant on all issues, but it does provide evidence that the findings of the consultancy have been taken seriously.

The commitment of international development agencies to improving learning is put to the test in their use of consultancies. Consultancy inputs provide ideal opportunities for a concentrated collection of experience and learning, and this can be achieved if adequate time and attention are invested in the feedback period and evaluation of consultancy inputs. However, clients and consultants in our survey seemed to be united in believing that more value could be extracted from consultancy inputs, and in regretting that too often reports and the hard work that went into them are not adequately used. One explanation offered for this state of affairs is that new and urgent priorities intervene and make reading the report seem less urgent, so it is not read for some time after it has been written.

The responsibility remains with the client to see that recommend-ations are discussed, assessed, and then taken forward as appropriate. When consultants and clients work together on implementation, it is normally through a 'process supporter' model of consultancy (see Chapter 3). This means that the consultant remains in touch with the client throughout the implementation of change and takes a more effective form of responsibility for his or her work.

Much consultancy work in the international development sector still takes the form of rapid, one-off inputs. This means that extra effort is required to capture learning from each consultancy. It would help if consultancy managers were systematically required to summarise key learning and implications from particular exercises, and their summaries were circulated as appropriate. This might focus on identifying learning and compensate for the perceived need to move on as a matter of urgency to new work. Some organisations hold periodic reviews of consultancy work in order to identify major lessons coming out of it. This may be more common with evaluations than with other forms of consultancy input.

Despite clients' frequently stated desire to learn from consultancy work, there remains a reluctance to finance the small amount of extra time needed to make this a reality. It can help if learning is planned in, as an appropriately financed organisational objective.

Evaluation of the consultant's inputs

For the benefit of consultants, clients should ensure that their organisation produces a clear written reaction to consultancy findings. It should be a rule to give rapid feedback when a report is produced. For consultants it is better to receive feedback – however critical – than to be left in the dark.

> *'I heard nothing at all, and then six months later they phoned me up to ask a simple question about the work which made it obvious that they had not read the report.'*
> (A consultant)

Feedback is important for both clients and consultants. Time should be set aside for it when planning the consultancy. Some consultants to whom we spoke have tried to use questionnaires to get feedback on their work, but they have not been able to persist with them.

> *'I tried to offer a client a feedback opportunity by saying that I would invoice for one of the consultancy days six weeks after the main part of the consultancy had been completed. They would be able to claim a day of my time to discuss the effects of the consultancy or ask for some additional inputs in that time. They were not interested and seized on how I could do the main work in one less day than seemed reasonable before! I still think it was a good idea.'*
> (A consultant)

It is important to assess the role and performance of the consultant separately from the consultancy itself, because the outcome of the consultancy might be good despite poor performance by the consultant, or *vice versa*. The consultant may work hard and skilfully in an impossible situation (for example, where key information is not available) but then be blamed for poor results. The pressure on both consultant and client to move on to the next piece of work may mean that the level of analysis is not adequate to make a distinction between the work of the consultant and the overall results. This will make it difficult to extract key learning points and to avoid repeating poor work in the future.

It is also important for clients to allow consultants to comment on how the consultancy process was managed, so that future processes can be improved.

Management reactions to failure

The most difficult aspect of managing a consultancy is when the client finds the report, or other products, to be unsatisfactory. Although regular feedback throughout the consultancy is the ideal, it is not always possible to achieve it. Sometimes the nature of the work means that the client is presented with a consultancy product after very little involvement in the process. For example, a project review may be taking place in another country, or in a remote area where contact is difficult and communication has broken down.

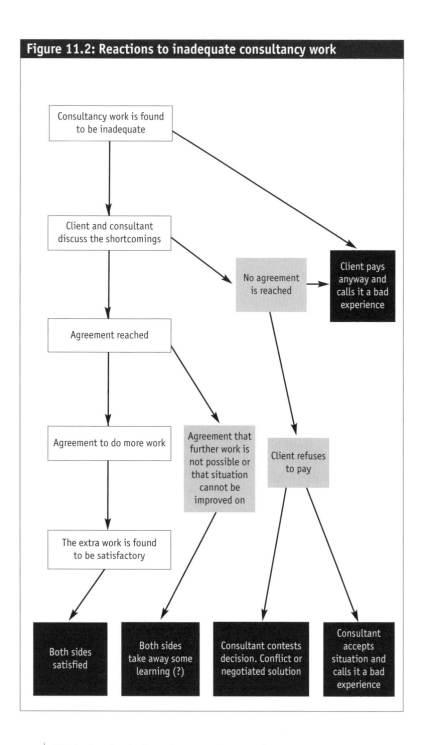

Figure 11.2: Reactions to inadequate consultancy work

Consultancy work is found to be inadequate

Client and consultant discuss the shortcomings

No agreement is reached

Client pays anyway and calls it a bad experience

Agreement reached

Agreement to do more work

Agreement that further work is not possible or that situation cannot be improved on

Client refuses to pay

The extra work is found to be satisfactory

Both sides satisfied

Both sides take away some learning (?)

Consultant contests decision. Conflict or negotiated solution

Consultant accepts situation and calls it a bad experience

Figure 11.2 shows a range of possible reactions to the apparent failure of a consultancy. Only a few of them are genuinely satisfactory to all parties. Too often the result is that one or both parties are dissatisfied, but they feel obliged to accept the situation as a bad experience. A lot of poor work gets written off, but this leads to bad reputations for consultants and for consultancy in general, bad learning, and bad projects.

In some situations, it may be possible to repair the damage, or for the consultant to provide additional inputs so that the end result is satisfactory to both parties. However, the consultant may not be willing to do extra work without extra pay, or may simply not be available to make good the shortcomings. There are also situations in which it is simply not possible to repair a piece of work or to do it over again. In such situations, both parties are obliged to accept the failure – although perhaps they will learn valuable lessons from the experience.

Participatory work and capacity strengthening

We end this chapter by considering two dimensions of consultancy work that are valued especially highly in the international development sector: participation and capacity building.

The most important people to meet in a consultancy are often partners at the community level. The IFRC handbook on monitoring and evaluation[16] sets out a range of sources for data collection and analysis, scoring them on their relative complexity and cost. It concludes that secondary sources are cheaper and less complex to use than primary sources, while beneficiary interviews using participatory methods are the most complex and costly sources of data. But clients often insist on a participatory style of consultancy without allocating realistic resources of time and money to it. Interviews and discussions at the grassroots level require careful planning and timing. Consultants should be honest about what can and cannot be done, and clients should adjust the scope of the project accordingly – or admit that participation cannot be achieved, given the resources available.

When the consultancy requires local visits, specific arrangements are necessary to ensure that consultants meet a range of community members (women and men, young and old, and different ethnic groups, etc.) in a way that is sensitive to their normal commitments. For example, women are often overloaded with domestic work and income earning and cannot easily spare time for interviews during the day; herders may not come to the village where meetings are taking place; and so on. Sometimes it is necessary for the consultant to stay overnight and make special journeys to meet the key people whose views will determine the future of the work. Local logistics should be considered, and time built in for debriefing at each site where the consultancy takes place, so that consultants can provide feedback to communities with whom they have worked.

> 'We were meant to be looking at the impact of the work on the most marginalised people in the area. Every time we located their houses (which tended to be the farthest away from the point where we were dropped off) and sat down and got a good rapport going, the driver would come and chase us, saying that the rest of the team were ready to leave. In the end I requested a separate vehicle so that we could do our work calmly.'
>
> (A consultant)

Consultants need to ask exactly what is meant by 'participatory' in a particular context, and assess just how flexible the client can be in responding to the results of participatory processes. Will it be possible to reorganise and refocus work if new directions and priorities emerge? In reality, it may be very difficult to hand over power (the ultimate goal of truly participatory development work) when donors insist on strict timetables and predetermined priorities.

The most difficult cases usually involve project design, where some features of the work are fixed (for example, the delivery of health care or water supply), but there is a desire to involve the participants in the details of the plans. The consultant may be put in a difficult situation if there is no clear distinction between what is fixed and what can be determined by participatory methods. For instance, if a consultant is hired to carry out staff training, some aspects of that training should be adjusted to take account of the participants' needs as they emerge during the event.

> 'They had asked me to run a participatory training programme with staff, but on the first day, before I had met any of the staff, they wanted to know what would be in the timetable for each day!'
>
> (A consultant)

Capacity building

One of the objectives of a consultancy may be to help to build an organisation's capacity to achieve its vision and mission. The consultancy may focus on assessing the structure and functioning of the organisation, in order to adjust them to meet current needs. Or it may focus on building the capacity of an array of local organisations to engage with local government. But there is also much talk of building the capacity of consultants: donors or INGOs may seek to equip nationally based consultants to respond to their requirements.

However, clients' rhetoric is not always matched by their actual investment in the consultancy. It is over-optimistic to assume that a mixed team of consultants (international and national) working together on a short-term assignment will necessarily learn from one another. If capacity strengthening is a clear objective of the work, then time needs to be factored in for reflection on the process, and for the exchange of experience and even identification of further needs for support.

As aid agencies' management decisions are increasingly decentralised, and consultants in their turn establish themselves in the countries and regions where assignments are based, it is possible that there will be more structured support for local consultancy capacity. There have been some initiatives to provide national consultants with information and tools to enable them to provide services to donors and international agencies. In Brazil and Nigeria, for example, the British government's Department for International Development has funded projects to train local consultants and provide equipment on loan for assignments. But international agencies must recognise that these national consultants have much to teach them about different methodological approaches and other ways of working.

12 | Ethical concerns

This chapter considers the implications of the fact that consultancy is largely unregulated by employment law or institutional rules. For these reasons, several issues of good practice depend on the personal motivation and self-discipline of the individuals involved – both consultants and client/managers – and are therefore ethical issues.

Clients and consultants in the international development sector must be scrupulous in their dealings with each other: fair about money matters, fair about sharing information, and jointly committed to doing a good job and advancing the work in the best interests of the communities who might benefit. Consultants should be transparent in their dealings with the client and give the client value for money. Clients should aim to work always in the best interests of their partners and to deal fairly and transparently with consultants. These principles give rise to the issues that are presented in this chapter.

Professional conduct

Conflicts of interest

Both commissioners and consultants need to guard against conflicts of interest. For example, a client might ask a consultant to evaluate work that he or she had helped to design or carry out. It is often the case that the consultant has good knowledge of the work to be evaluated. On the strength of his or her previous contacts and experience, the consultant may be approached to undertake the assignment. In this case the consultant should refuse the contract but offer to act as a key informant to the person who does carry out the work.

Being seen to avoid conflicts of interest is as important as actually doing so. A good consultant might be able to do an objective evaluation of work in which he or she had previously been involved, but the consultancy may not be seen to be independent, and that perception could reduce or completely negate its value.

> 'They asked me to evaluate the results of work, although I had provided a training input in the early stages. I pointed out that there was a conflict of interest .... They replied that they wanted me to do the evaluation, because I knew the situation and understood their organisation. I did the work but did not look at the training component and I put a warning note in the introduction to my report.'
> (A consultant)

Where consultants perceive a conflict between the best interests of a client and the best interests of the partners or beneficiaries of the client's work, they should raise this fact with the client. The client would be bound by professional ethics to address the problem as transparently and objectively as possible.

Commenting on members of staff

Consultants often find themselves in the privileged position of being able to talk to staff and learn about the workings of an agency in ways that may not be possible for managers. It may be tempting then for managers to ask consultants for their views on the staff concerned. This is not ethical. First, the agency should have its own staff-review mechanisms that do not rely on casual observations by external consultants. Second, the staff must know how and when they are being assessed by their agency: their work should not be analysed without their being made aware of it.

However, a consultant could of course be hired to do assessments of staff under the terms of an open, specific consultancy. Such an explicit appraisal of staff is legitimate and is not the subject of our concern, which is the use of a consultancy for covert assessments when it is supposed to be focused on other work.

Commenting on other consultants

Similar ethical considerations might need to be applied when a consultant is put in the position of assessing the work of a paid supplier of services to the client, although he or she was not hired to do this. The problem could also arise where a consultant was hired to work on a programme but was asked to comment on the work of another consultant who had previously worked on the programme. Consultants should avoid making comments if they find themselves being drawn into this type of situation.

Revealing and protecting sources

Confidentiality is another potentially difficult matter. When interviewing members of staff, in order to encourage the most frank expression of views, the consultant should assure them that their comments will be treated in confidence. This would later prevent the consultant from identifying particular staff members as the origin of the remarks. In fact, this is good practice even where staff had no specific reason to believe that their observations were made in confidence.

The ethical point is that the consultant has been hired to carry out a survey of staff opinions, not to report on specific individuals. Difficulties may arise when the consultant has to report to the client views that managers may find displeasing or unacceptable. They may ask the consultant 'Who said that?', or 'Where did you get that idea?' The consultant should make it clear to the client and to each interviewee that interviews will be run according to a code of conduct that protects the confidentiality of the interviewee. If someone wants the consultant to know something but does not wish the consultant to use the information at all, he or she would need to make this clear.

Sensitive material

Consultants are often required to examine sensitive material, or they may discover sensitive material in the course of carrying out a consultancy. Simple examples would be the spending pattern of the client agency, or the internal politics of the organisation. It is vital that such information is treated in confidence by consultants. Of course, contracts normally include a clause stating that information obtained during a consultancy cannot be disclosed by the consultant to a third party, or certainly not without prior written permission. However, it is extremely unlikely that any such matter would become a legal issue, and consultants are required to act in good faith, using their judgement to decide what should reasonably be considered confidential, and what can be safely disclosed.

If consultants discover evidence of corruption, misconduct, or negligence, they are under an ethical obligation to report it, even though this could cause serious problems. Clients should explain the mechanisms that are in place for reporting suspected malpractice and they should investigate all such reports.

Professional integrity

Realistic claims and realistic expectations

Consultants who are trying to get work are in the process of selling themselves, but they must not make false claims about their abilities or experience. Nor should they misrepresent the potential usefulness of a piece of work: instead they should give their frank opinion about what can be achieved. In a competitive market it is tempting to exaggerate what you can do. Similarly clients should not oversell the piece of work by hiding difficulties or being over-optimistic about the potential of the consultancy or the project.

The negotiations at the start of the consultancy should include a process of mutual management of expectations, as both client and consultant explore what they would like to be able to do – and what they can realistically do.

The power of the expert consultant

Consultants may find themselves in situations where they have more experience or greater expertise or higher qualifications than the client/manager with whom they are working. Responsible consultants should use their competencies to support clients, resisting any temptation to impose their views. Where the client and the consultant have worked to develop a good relationship, this is less likely to happen.

Professional respect

Consultants, especially solo freelance consultants, get their job security from two things: their network of contacts and their reputation. They get work because they are known, and because people speak highly of the quality of their work. Consultants work hard to maintain their networks and their reputations. Building a reputation is like rolling up a ball of string: it takes many small bits of work to build it up, but one slip can cause a large amount to unravel.

Clients need to be aware of this when commenting on the work of a consultant. One small remark may be enough to damage a reputation that will take a long time to repair. If a client feels that a piece of work has not gone well, it is tempting to blame the consultant. A poorly phrased remark could ruin the reputation of a consultant for a long time after the event has been forgotten by the client. The problem can be managed by good reviews of each piece of consultancy work, and considered comments on the consultant's work – comments as careful as those contained in a reference for an employee.

Similar ethical behaviour is required of consultants, who should not risk damaging the reputation of other consultants by commenting unnecessarily on their work or qualifications. Consultants must never defame another consultant, although the temptation may be great during a highly competitive tendering process. We would suggest the following rules.

- Do not offer a view on the professional competencies of a consultant, unless you are expressly asked to do so.
- Before speaking about another consultant, find out why you are being asked to give comments: have you been named as a referee, for example?

- When obliged to comment on another consultant, be factual and specific about particular work that the consultant did, rather than offering vague general opinions.

Follow-on work

If a consultant has obtained a contract through a consultancy organisation or a third party (for example, another consultant), he or she should refer any follow-up work back to the source of the first contract. It is very common for a client to ask a consultant to do a second consultancy; in such a case, the source of the first contract has a reasonable claim on the follow-on work. This is particularly important if a consultant is unavailable to do a piece of work and recommends another consultant who does the work and is then offered some follow-on work. A responsible consultant in this situation should remind the client of the prior contact with the first consultant and should inform the first consultant of the offer of further work.

Recognising responsibility for results

Consultancy work requires both sides to take an active role in pursuing good results and making themselves accountable for success. All kinds of variable factors affect the outcome of consultancies, many of them beyond the control of those taking part, and it may be tempting to blame circumstances for poor results. There are situations where it is possible to avoid hard work without anyone else knowing about it, but responsible consultants and clients should make the extra effort, even though it will not be acknowledged by anyone else.

> 'It was getting late and time to leave. We had done about 20 interviews when a woman arrived, saying she'd heard that we wanted to talk to people. The local consultant thanked her and started the interview. No one would ever know or mind if we did 20 interviews or 21, but she just did the job. I was very impressed.'
> (A consultant)

Ultimate responsibility

One certainty that cannot be avoided is the fact that the final responsibility for the success or failure of a consultancy rests with the client. However badly the consultant has performed, the client is ultimately responsible for the management of the process. Perhaps the consultancy manager should have identified a better consultant, perhaps he or she should have monitored the progress more closely, and perhaps he or she failed to give enough attention to ensuring that the logistics were in place so that everything ran smoothly. It can be too easy to put all the blame for a failed piece of work on to the consultant – particularly if the findings are not to the liking of the client.

Finally ...

Responsible consultants should try to promote skill-sharing, mentoring, training, and participatory and inclusive approaches, to make it more likely that the organisation can manage similar situations without further consultancy inputs.

13 | Being a consultant

This chapter is primarily intended for people who are considering working as consultants. It may also help people who currently work as consultants to reflect on their work. We hope it will also help clients to form a better understanding of the situations in which consultants tend to work, especially the constraints under which they operate.

Being a consultant

The following are typical questions and concerns raised with us by practising and aspiring consultants in the international development sector:

- *What's it like working on your own?*
- *What fees can I charge?*
- *What expenses can I expect to charge?*
- *What insurance should I have?*
- *Should I be a sole trader, or set up a company?*
- *Do I need an accountant?*
- *Will I get enough work?*

Working as a consultant can mean operating on a freelance, self-employed basis; or working on the staff of a consultancy company, with accompanying employment benefits. We will not look in detail at the latter way of working: we focus instead on the situation of those who work as self-employed solo consultants. In this case, people are free to work for any client that they choose, either hired directly by the organisation that is seeking the consultancy services, or else sub-contracted by a third party, for example a consultancy company, for the duration of the assignment.

How do people become consultants?

As international development agencies decentralise their operations, there is an increasing trend towards contracting consultants locally and regionally – which creates a market for individuals who are able to respond to this demand. In some situations people combine full-time jobs in academic institutions, government, or NGOs with an occasional consultancy assignment. Most consultants in our survey did not directly choose to set themselves up as consultants. It seems very common for people to start by treating consultancy as a temporary stage in their careers, while searching for other employment. Many then find that they like working as a consultant and they stop looking for other work.

No formal training is required in order to start work as a consultant in this sector, but since one of the qualities that clients are buying is knowledge and understanding, it is hard to imagine someone setting up as a consultant at a very early stage of his or her career.

> '(Just because) someone was a good staff member does not mean they will be a good consultant. There are real skills involved, and few people have them.'
> (An NGO manager)

Working as a consultant is different from being a staff member, in ways that may not be immediately apparent. People starting out as consultants have to find this out for themselves, because there is no standard induction process. In fact, new consultants have to learn to do everything for themselves: they must do their own promotion, make all their own financial arrangements, and provide their own office infrastructure.

> 'My first steps into consultancy were "a very steep learning curve", which is code for being dropped head-first into responsibilities, ethical dilemmas, financial insecurity, and a new pattern of work without support or guidance. I was lucky with the client, the receivers, and my fellow team members, who were all supportive. In this way I rode out the assault on my confidence and the possible threat to my reputation at the outset.'
> (A consultant)

It is essential to talk to people who are already working freelance and learn from their experience. Professional advice will almost certainly be needed on matters such as legal and financial liabilities, tax, and national insurance contributions. What insurance does a consultant need? What basic equipment is needed for a functioning office? These issues are touched on in Chapters 9 and 10 of this book. Here we will simply offer some miscellaneous pieces of advice:

- Build up a cash-flow fund for paying taxes and surviving the periods when work is scarce. (Some clients take a long time to pay.)
- Buy a good laptop computer, the best you can afford. This is the most important tool of your trade.
- Obtain and keep receipts for all business-related expenditure. You will need them if you want to claim the expenditure against tax.

Coping with uncertainty

'A good consultant? Well, a lot comes down to personality.'
(A client)

The life of a freelance consultant is often insecure. He or she must be able to cope with times when work is scarce, and there are no potential assignments on the horizon. Especially in the first year or two, income flow will be a cause for concern. There will be other times when there is too much work, and the consultant has to refuse work that is both interesting and lucrative.

One way to cope with times when work is lacking, or less intense, is to have some other projects that can be done unpaid at any time. The time could be used for routine administrative tasks (doing the accounts, renewing stationery stocks, etc.); but it could also be used for writing articles or receiving some training, learning about new computer software, and so on. It is a good time for producing better versions of training materials, and similar investments in the quality of one's own work.

'That year was the first time I had a real "hole" in work, and I was worried about money. We cancelled a holiday... It was also the year in which I published two articles.'
(A consultant)

Most consultants enjoy the unpredictable nature of their work and relish the diversity of the engagements that they carry out. But it is easy to see how the same characteristics can seem unattractive to others, who might see consultancy as an insecure and fragmented form of career.

Consultancy work in the international development sector

Even when a contract has been awarded, a degree of uncertainty remains. The work is often based in difficult and remote locations; situations are unpredictable, and the consultant will have to accept changes at the last minute. The consultant must be able to adapt rapidly to all the unplanned changes and deliver good-quality work despite them all.

Travel will often be uncomfortable and exhausting. Consultants working in rural and poor urban areas, and making frequent international journeys by air, are exposed to considerable health risks. It is sometimes hard to admit to being unwell or overtired, and there is often pressure to avoid appearing weak.

> *'She arrived from the airport and said she was tired and was going to the hotel to sleep and would continue work tomorrow. I was terribly impressed, I don't think I would have dared do that.'*
> (A consultant speaking about another consultant)

Self-promotion

Consultants need to be happy to promote themselves to clients. Some may find this difficult. Several people in our survey expressed the view that women in particular may tend to undersell themselves, and clients should be aware of this. The chances of being hired for a particular job depend greatly on professional reputation and personal contacts. This means that consultants have to promote their expertise and their personality; they themselves are the 'product' that they are trying to sell. This way of working may not suit some personalities.

The curriculum vitae (CV) is the key tool used by consultants who are seeking work. Chapter 7 explains in detail how clients use CVs to assess consultants. Consultants need to have several up-to-date versions of their CV, in several formats, at all times.

Calculating fees

After the uncertainty of getting contracts, the second biggest concern mentioned by consultants in our survey was the fixing of fees and ensuring a reasonable income. The exercise based on the 'one-per-cent rule', presented in Chapter 9, is one way of working out what you would need to charge for the number of days that you would like to work.

Ask other consultants what fees they are currently receiving. Many consultants are defensive about such information, but some will give you an estimate of what they earn. Clients tend to say that they have fixed limits, but in fact they will very often negotiate. Consultants need to be able to negotiate about money in a clear and straightforward way, in an environment where there are persistent assumptions that consultants are overpaid. During a negotiation about fees, never try to explain why you need to charge the daily rate that you are asking for.

Certificates of qualifications

Certain donors and official agencies (the European Union, for example) require documentary evidence of formal academic and professional qualifications. Consultants should ensure that they keep their certificates safe and have a few copies ready for immediate use if they need to bid for work at short notice. Some agencies require copies of certificates to be accompanied by a statement (signed by the consultant or by a notary or other independent witness) to confirm that they are genuine, and it is certainly worth having some of these statements on file and ready for use.

Choosing work or being reactive

The work of consultants is essentially reactive. Although consultants do sometimes propose and promote bits of work and seek funding for specific initiatives or research projects, most assignments in the sector come from responding to enquiries and requests from clients. Overall, consultants do not control the work that they do; they may have to accept work that they do not particularly like, if other options are not available. People considering a career in consultancy should not imagine that they will always be able to choose the types of project, the types of intervention, or the particular places in which they will work.

Consultants are advised to review their work on a regular basis (say, once a year) and assess the degree of satisfaction that they have gained from the range of assignments on which they have worked. To seek out new types of work means extending one's networks and making new links that might lead to suitable offers. This takes time, because every contract is likely to lead to more work of a similar kind.

'Bellman' time

Self-employed consultants may risk working too much and being over-committed. One way to manage this problem is to follow the advice of Geoff Bellman, who has been a consultant for more than thirty years. In his book *The Consultant's Calling*, Bellman suggests that personal time is so important that it should be given the highest priority and put into the calendar of a consultant before all other commitments: *'make time for yourself your top priority. Not close to the top, but top'*... *'give it the same dignity as all those other meetings and activities you regularly note there'*. His choice of the word *dignity* is deliberate and very telling.

But what to do when a potential client asks if a consultant is available at a time that he or she has set aside as 'personal time'? The consultant is advised to say that he or she will be busy at that time and offer alternative dates. If the client seems unable or unwilling to be flexible, then the consultant should promise to see if it would be possible to rearrange personal commitments. If this proves to be possible, the consultant should call back and inform the client. However, this should not be done without fixing new dates for personal time. When consultants work too much, they stop enjoying their assignments and produce work of lower quality – which further limits their job satisfaction. If the overwork continues, especially in stressful situations, it can lead to serious health problems and damage personal relationships.

The importance of networks and maintaining contacts

'You will get most of your work by word of mouth, directly from clients, or via other consultants who have been offered work that they can't do. Keep in touch, and return favours.'
(Consultant)

Every consultant needs a good network of contacts, in order to hear about new opportunities, to be recommended for work by fellow consultants, and to engage in professional discussions. A network of contacts, not all of whom need to be consultants, can replace some of the social and professional functions of relationships with colleagues in a workplace. A 'network' may be as simple as a group of people with common interests, meeting for lunch once a month!

'You will be asked to dig deep into your own intellectual and emotional resources to develop the design, build trust with project workers, and write the report. It can be lonely, often with no-one you can develop ideas with.'
(A consultant)

Some people find that working as a consultant is unsatisfactory because informal support networks are not an adequate substitute for regular interactions with colleagues in an institution.

Professional development and continued learning

Consultants need to invest in their own professional development and prevent themselves from becoming stale and using the same material or methods for successive assignments. By belonging to professional associations, attending conferences, workshops, or gatherings of associates, one is also maintaining and developing networks and promoting oneself. Consultants should plan to set aside two weeks (ten working days) for their own professional development each year, and should expect to pay for some of this.

It is possible to share work with other consultants as a way of sharing learning. It can be very helpful to ask another consultant to review a report or a proposed design for an intervention. The consultant who has won the contract could pay the other a small sum to provide this support. This sharing of work could be developed into a more formal system whereby parts of an assignment are subcontracted, so that more than one consultant is working on the job for a significant period of time; but such an arrangement should be approved by the client. Most contracts make subcontracting rather difficult, even though the result for the client might be a piece of work of higher quality.

Getting feedback

Getting feedback from clients is a useful element in improving performance, but it requires special efforts and sympathetic responses from clients.

> 'The downside [of working as a consultant] is never really knowing what happened next, and what value your work had ... I did try to get this kind of feedback from clients, but it was only really possible where I had a pre-existing good relationship – otherwise, why would they spend the time, unless there was an ongoing relationship?'
> (A consultant)

One way of learning is to receive feedback on tenders or approaches that were unsuccessful. Sometimes this is offered spontaneously by the client, but most often it is not. Some consultants actively try to get feedback about their work by talking to a client after completing the assignment, and by sending feedback forms. This was valued by a number of the clients in our survey, but there is no uniformity of practice and no commitment to this kind of learning.

Promoting learning

One of the negative aspects of external consultancies is the perception among members of staff that much of the learning from an exercise walks away with consultants at the end of the assignment. Conversely, consultants can only suggest ways in which learning can be promoted within the client organisation. They cannot compensate for the absence of a learning culture in particular institutional contexts. So what can consultants do to promote learning from the work that they have done?

*'The client contacted me and asked if I could help with a project
evaluation and perhaps suggest someone for another similar evaluation
in the same country. I said that I would do one of the evaluations and
that a close colleague would do the other, so that there was some
consistency between the two bits of work. I also suggested that we should
then run a workshop for both project teams to develop plans for the
future of both projects. I was surprised when they agreed, because it
might have seemed like we were trying to make more work out of the
contract. The additional workshop did lead to learning between the
different teams and headquarters staff. ...I have only ever managed to
get one client to agree to this kind of double input, although I thought it
was ethical and valuable.'*
(A consultant)

Consultants should seek to persuade clients to invest in better learning:
for example, by allocating time for feedback, and by recording the lessons
from the consultancy. Clients might be encouraged to develop short
versions of consultancy reports which do not compromise confidentiality
or staff security but allow the lessons of the consultancy to be shared more
widely. Some agencies produce evaluation briefs, for example, which
contain only the key information about the project, together with the main
learning points. The briefs can be shared within the agency, among staff
of other similar agencies, and with the public. Some consultants, with the
agreement of clients, write articles synthesising experience for wider
sharing through conferences and journals. Writing reports or journal
articles could be a project for quiet times when work is not available.

Promoting high standards

As a consultant, you have to demonstrate high levels of integrity, and there
are sometimes no checks or safeguards to ensure this, apart from your
own standards. Consultants have to develop good relations with people
from a wide range of backgrounds at short notice, and balance the needs
of the multiple stakeholders involved in each job. Good communications
skills are important, but being honest and transparent are also key
qualities: personal integrity is an important criterion for the selection of
consultants.

Give consulting a fair trial

You may know immediately if you do not like the life of a consultant, but
it may take some time – perhaps a couple of years – to experience enough
of the reality to make a realistic judgement. In the first year, work is likely
to come through your immediate networks and previous employment.

Your networks will expand quickly, but initially work will tend to come from relatively few contacts. At some stage in the first two years, any new freelance consultant is likely to experience the problems of both under-employment and over-commitment. This is the real test of whether you are suited to the life of a consultant, or whether you find the uncertainties unsettling and distracting; and whether or not you like having to construct and maintain your own informal networks, rather than working alongside colleagues in a formal setting. You will know if you are happy to organise your own training and professional development, rather than belonging to an institution which provides or supports such things. You may find that you are disturbed by a lack of organisational support and lack of career structure. However, if you find that you enjoy the freedom from institutional politics, and you appreciate the opportunity to focus entirely on a single piece of work, you may be suited to the work and lifestyle of consulting.

14 | Checklists for managers

In this chapter we present the seven key stages involved in a typical consultancy. For each stage we offer a checklist that consists of questions for managers. Not all consultancies need to go through all these steps. Shorter and simpler assignments may take some short cuts. Consultants and other stakeholders (for example, groups who may be receiving a visit from consultants) may want to work through the list to check what questions they might need to be asking at different stages.

1. Identifying and agreeing the need for a consultancy

1 Identify the need
- Are you sure that commissioning a consultancy is not an attempt to avoid a difficult management decision?
- Are you sure that this work cannot be done effectively by staff?
- What do you need: extra skills, experience, extra capacity, an independent view, or several of these?

2 Justify the need – prepare a written brief
- What would be the consequences of not doing this work?
- Can you write down the expected results and benefits?

3 Do a rough costing and identify financial resources
- Roughly how much will the consultancy cost? Estimate the number of days needed. Multiply by a relatively high daily rate. Add 20 per cent for costs. Then add another 10 per cent for contingencies.
- Where can you find this amount of money?

4 Consult key stakeholders
- Who will be directly affected by the consultancy?
- Whom do you need to involve in planning the work?

5 Check policies and procedures and seek necessary approvals
- Have you checked your organisation's policies and procedures for hiring consultants?
- Is it likely that you will have to go through a formal process of tendering?
- If so, have you factored this into the schedule?

2. Planning the consultancy

1 Agree who will be the manager of consultancy
- Do you know who will actually manage the consultancy on a day-to-day basis?
- Do you know who will provide administrative support to the process?
- Are these people aware of this proposal?

2 Draw up a timeline for the whole process
- Can you produce a timeline from beginning to end of the consultancy?
- If you add 50 per cent more time, is there still enough time to do the consultancy?
- What events could disturb the running of the consultancy? For example: public holidays, religious festivals, staff holidays, staff contracts, change of weather or season, elections.
- How long can the consultancy be delayed and still be effective?
- Have you allowed sufficient time for consultation on the ToR, initial team building, genuine participation at the community level, and feedback and learning at the end of the consultancy?

3 Prepare Terms of Reference
- Do you know who will draft the ToR?
- Has this person read Chapter 6 of this book (concerning the contents of ToR)?

4 Review sources of information

5 Circulate Terms of Reference and consult stakeholders

6 Draw up a budget
- Do you have an overall figure for the budget?
- Can you do detailed costings for the consultancy?
- Have you calculated what you can afford to pay in consultancy fees?
- Will fees be paid on a daily-rate basis or as a lump sum?
- Do you know if you should pay in several instalments?
- Have you calculated how much you will need to spend on additional items? For example: international and local travel, accommodation, subsistence, meetings, translators, administrative support. Anything else?

7 Set criteria for selection of consultant(s)
- Can you describe the skills and experience required of the consultant(s)?
- Can you sort them into essential and desirable criteria?
- Do you know if other stakeholders have other criteria for selection of consultants?
- Do you know where to start looking for consultants, and whom to ask for suggestions?

8 Decide the basis and method of payment

9 Begin preparation of materials /logistics/ preliminary studies
- Can the consultant(s) obtain all the necessary background documents?
- Will the consultant(s) be able to meet all the appropriate people?
- How will the consultant(s) obtain additional information as it becomes necessary?

3. Finding consultants, scouting, and negotiating

1 Identify potential consultants
- How will you find consultants for this work?
- Will it be clear to everyone that the selection was unbiased?
- Have you considered seeking out consultants not previously known to the organisation?

2 Contact, interview, assess capability of candidates
- Do the consultants whom you have contacted have a clear idea of the purpose of the assignment?
- Have you made it clear what skills and experience are required to know whether or not they are well suited for the work?
- Do they know enough about the timetable to be able to assess their availability?

3 Conduct initial scouting
- Do the consultants' CVs give you enough information about their skills and experience?
- Do you know what questions you need to ask them to be sure that they have the necessary competencies?

4 Initiate a tendering process
- Do you need to go through a tendering process because the job is of sufficient size to require it?
- Who will be involved in any tendering process (or in any other process of selection)?
- Are there other consultants whom you can approach if the first choice turns out to be unavailable?

5 Decide to proceed
- Have you made it clear to the candidates how and when decisions will be made about the consultancy?

4. Negotiating and contracting: developing the relationship

1 **Interview consultants/tenderers**

2 **Negotiate Terms of Reference/terms and conditions**
   - Do you know how much freedom you have to negotiate on fees?
   - Do you understand how consultants calculate their daily rates?
   - Do you think you can reach a fair and acceptable agreement on fees?
   - Is it clear to you and the consultant(s) how much will be paid in fees?
   - Is it clear to you and to the consultant(s) what expenses will be covered, and by what means?

3 **Agree roles and responsibilities**
   - Has the consultancy manager informed the successful candidate(s) that the award of the contract means that there is now a commitment to carry out the work?
   - Is it clear to you and the successful candidate(s) which elements of the ToR are negotiable?
   - Have any changes that were made during the discussions been ratified in writing?

4 **Award the contract**

5 **Give feedback to other candidates**
   - Have you explained to the unsuccessful candidates why they were not chosen?

5. Preparatory consultancy work

1 Assemble background material for the consultant(s)
- Have you supplied the necessary briefing materials to the consultant(s)?

2 Prepare the logistics
- Have travel arrangements been made?
- Have accommodation and venues been booked?
- Is it clear who is responsible for providing further information and logistical support for the consultants?

3 Confirm details of the consultancy management and contact schedules
- Do you know when the consultant(s) will report on progress?
- Do you have a schedule of times for direct contact with them?
- Do you know how to contact the consultant(s) if the reporting arrangements fail?
- Are the identities of the manager and the other clients (if any) clear to the consultant(s)?

4 Consult stakeholders about the schedule
- Is it clear who the main stakeholders are?
- Have all the stakeholders (in the client organisation, the partner organisation(s), the communities, etc.) who may be contacted or inconvenienced by the consultancy been informed about the work?
- Have all these stakeholders agreed to give time to the consultancy?

6. The core consultancy

1 Induction and briefing
- Have you set aside time for an induction meeting? Will there be enough time for socialising and getting to know each other, as well as the business of the meeting?
- Have you thoroughly briefed the consultant(s) about your organisation and its values and ways of working?
- Will the briefing be seen as fair and unbiased by everyone in the organisation?
- Have you presented any important internal political issues without prejudicing the process?

2 Team meetings/training/clarification of responsibilities
- Have you confirmed and agreed what the organisation is expected to provide in terms of administrative support, and what the consultant(s) will have to provide or pay for independently?
- If you have commissioned a team of consultants, do you and the team leader know how you will deal with a member who fails to deliver?

3 Initial work
- Have security procedures and health and safety issues been clearly explained to the consultant(s)?

4 Inception meeting to clarify or modify ToR
- Have you discussed the ToR with the consultant(s), exchanged ideas, and reached a clear, shared understanding on the work to be done?

5 Information collection
- Have you checked that the consultant(s) can get access to the people and the documents they need?
- Is there sufficient flexibility for the consultant(s) to include other interviews?

6 Regular review of progress/modifications of scope
- Are you prepared for the possibility that the full ToR cannot be implemented, and that some elements of the work may have to be dropped?
- Do you know what can be left out without preventing the consultancy achieving its most important objectives?
- Can you or the consultant(s) compensate for information that cannot be obtained, or interviews that cannot be held?

7 Analysis of findings/initial judgements
- Have you agreed how the consultant(s) can report initial findings?
- Have you identified mechanisms for exchanging ideas (for example, e-mails, short presentations, etc.) so that there are no surprises at the end of the consultancy?

8 Final assessments/recommendations
- Will there be enough time for the consultant(s) to analyse and think through their observations before presenting their findings?
- Can the stakeholders respond to the initial findings so that the consultant(s) can make good use of their feedback?

9 Report and summary
- Have you defined and agreed the format, size, and contents of the final report?
- Have you allowed enough time for drafting the report?
- Will there be time within the contract to obtain comments from all the interested parties and to produce a final report?

7. Finalisation and follow-up

1 Approve the final draft of the report and close the contract
- Have you formally approved the final report?
- Have you approved the final payment, or authorised others to make it?

2 Decide on action in response to the recommendations
- Have you decided which recommendations your organisation can accept, which it needs to modify, and which it has to reject?

3 Act on the recommendations
- How will you respond to the recommendations?
- Can the consultant(s) redraft those recommendations that are too difficult to implement?

4 Give feedback to the consultant(s)
- Have you discussed with the consultant(s) what went well and what might have gone better?
- Have you told the consultant(s) about any weaknesses in the work and given them the chance to respond and, if appropriate, offer to do more work or make good the work done?
- Can the consultant(s) improve their work in the future on the basis of feedback that you have provided?

5 Evaluate changes made as a result of the consultancy
- Have you set aside time to assess the overall impact of the consultancy?
- Can you assess the changes that have been brought about by the consultancy?
- Can you share the main learning points with colleagues within your organisation?
- Can you share the learning outside the organisation?
- Do you know who else should learn the lessons from this consultancy (inside and outside your organisation)?

15 | Conclusion

In this chapter we re-visit the three key areas of **context**, **management**, and **relationships** as they affect consultancy work, and we consider some potential trends in the use of consultancies.

Context

Although it is not easy to find hard evidence, there is general agreement among those whom we consulted that NGOs working in development have significantly increased their use of consultants during the past decade or so. The demand for consultants is greater than ever, and so is the supply. We assume that this will continue to be the case, even though there may be changes in how consultancies are managed and conducted.

Many organisations pay for consultancy services across a range of budgets, and assign their management to a wide range of staff. As a result, the agencies that we consulted were not able to quantify changes in the numbers of commissions or the sums of money spent. Nevertheless, most people think that the use of consultants will continue to increase, and that the reasons for recent increases are still relevant.

A general trend towards using consultants

People who write about management in organisations and the changing nature of employment have suggested for a long time that long-term employment is likely to become less common and the use of consultants more common. They have predicted that organisations will hire people on short contracts and use greater numbers of consultants, mostly in order to be more flexible.

Increased demands

We note three main reasons for the increasing demand for consultants in the NGO development sector: *financial factors*, the need for *flexibility*, and the demand for *increased rigour*.

The financial costs of employing permanent staff are likely to continue to increase. Hiring consultants may appear a cheaper option than having to pay increasing sums of money for insurance, pensions, equipment, and so on.

Employing people as consultants can increase an organisation's flexibility. Agencies need to be able to adapt to new situations and new markets. This relates to new types of work as much as to changes in their funding sources. Consultants can be brought in to work on new issues for a set period of time. Making permanent staff redundant or redeploying them if the nature of the organisation's work changes is a costly and complex business.

There is an increase in scrutiny and a demand for greater professionalism in the sector, in response to donors' requirement of greater rigour in funding proposals, and the consequent growth in demand for monitoring and evaluation for accountability and learning. Some smaller agencies in particular note an increased use of consultants for this latter purpose. There is some debate about what the push for greater 'professionalism' means in practice. Some commentators are concerned that it represents a change in values, rather than an improvement in the way that work is done. Nevertheless, people whom we consulted expressed the view that using consultants is certainly one way in which agencies, and particularly smaller ones with few if any specialised staff, can improve the quality of their work, and their capacity to present their work to donors.

As larger international NGOs increasingly devolve their functions away from their traditional headquarters through regionalisation or decentralisation, they add to the demand for regionally and locally recruited consultants. There may be a continuing demand for Northern-based consultants in some situations, but increasingly priority will be given to the hiring of local and national consultants.

Another shift concerns the type of organisation that is hiring consultants. This varies according to national context, but some donors are increasingly providing funds directly to their partners, including civil-society membership organisations, to enable them to contract consultancy support directly. Donors who previously funded NGO-support organisations now tend to pass their funds directly to those organisations' clients, and these clients are free to choose whom they will hire.

The supply of consultants

As agencies devolve their functions to other countries, and down-size some of their central offices, some of the redundant staff are moving into the supply of consultancy services. Public-sector re-structuring in both North and South also means that there is a bigger pool of people working as freelancers. Reduced funding for university departments in both Northern and Southern countries has put pressure on academics to seek work through providing consultancy services too.

More coherent capacity building

As we have noted in previous chapters, international agencies subscribe to the idea of building the capacity of national consultants to enable them to meet their needs. This has often taken the form of bringing together an international (frequently Northern) consultant with knowledge of (Northern) agency demands to work with local and national consultants to carry out a one-off piece of work. Somehow there is an expectation that knowledge will be shared, and as a result national consultants will better understand the requirements of these clients.

So far efforts to strengthen national consultancy capacity to respond to the needs of Northern agency clients has been somewhat sporadic and one-sided. It might be a better approach if various clients in different countries were to collaborate in developing local capacity. It would require clients to be open to listening more carefully to the concerns and capabilities of nationally based practitioners.

The focus of consultancy work

Consultancy work relating to clients' programmes will perhaps move away from a focus on projects and require an awareness of and contribution to policy issues, as international development increasingly involves an assessment of the impact of governance and public policy.

New donors

This book has been written with the traditional funding of development organisations in mind. It will be interesting to see how new national and corporate donors may shape the consultancy world in development.

Management

As we have shown, managing and participating in a consultancy process need the investment of staff time. A significant increase in the use of consultancies would require clients to be more efficient in the hiring and management of consultants. It is hard to imagine that the current methods of recruitment and management would be sufficient to cope with a large increase in the volume of consultancies. Clients would find it hard to find the time to recruit, brief, and manage more consultants if they had to organise the management of each consultancy input separately, as now.

One way to enable small numbers of staff to manage an increased number of consultancies would be to issue fewer, larger contracts to consultancy groups, instead of issuing a larger number of smaller contracts to individual consultants. This is what has happened to some extent in the commercial and statutory sectors. The administrative costs should be lower, and speed and flexibility might be increased. It would be possible to sign larger contracts with a small number of preferred suppliers of services. A number of suppliers could be asked to go through a pre-qualification process. The companies would be required to provide mixed teams of local and international consultants, as needed. Solo consultants would be unlikely to work directly with development agencies, but would work instead through the larger companies and groupings.

It could become more common practice for agencies to offer larger pieces of work. For example, a development agency could ask for all its projects that were due for evaluation to be evaluated by a single consultancy group. The group might provide different teams with different specialist skills for different projects, but it would provide a consistent approach and perhaps also improve learning between projects.

A change towards fewer and larger contracts could come about through consultants forming teams and offering to carry out a particular service, or to manage tasks such as a range of project evaluations. So far, consultancies have been almost always initiated by clients, but an offer from a competent group of consultants might be an opportunity to reduce the workload on staff and increase consistency over a range of jobs.

The quality of work done in consultancies could be improved if they were considered to be part of routine work that has to be planned and reported on like any other piece of work. We have noted that many of the problems encountered in consultancies are due to lack of time: not enough time for the planning and recruitment, not enough time for the core work, and not enough time to absorb and make use of the learning. It may be difficult to imagine all these difficulties being resolved at once, but some better use of time must come from including consultancy inputs in regular planning processes. (This apart, we recognise that there will always be situations that call for a piece of work at short notice to respond to particular circumstances.)

Consultancy styles

The purely 'technical' consultancy is likely to become rare. It is unlikely that consultants will be called on to deliver specialist input without engaging staff and stakeholders, and without working in a participatory style alongside them. Better planning should make it easier to allow the time needed for such approaches, particularly in relation to partners and community-level stakeholders.

Learning

Consultancies provide a valuable tool to help organisations to promote learning: learning about the specific work that is the subject of the consultancy, and learning about the process of the consultancy, providing evidence to put together with other learning from other similar studies. Yet the expectation that consultancy can by itself magically support an organisation to become a 'learning organisation' is not realistic. Organisations need to invest in systems, structures, and staff time to provide the framework for learning that is generated through consultancies. At the level of the specific consultancy, this means that allowing an extra day for bringing participants together to review findings, or bringing consultants together with staff to reflect on the actual process of work, or allowing time through the process so that consultants can actively share learning should be seen as acceptable use of resources, building in time for staff to synthesise and process the findings. These are small investments at this level which could make a positive difference. At the wider organisational level, the client organisation must have the systems in place that consultants can link into, so that the learning generated does not just merely walk away with the consultants, and they should ensure that material can be stored and is easily accessible later.

Relationships

Clients and consultants need to manage improvements in both the formal and informal aspects of consultancy work. They will need to be more attentive to the importance of good human relationships, and at the same time pay more attention to negotiating clear contractual arrangements. If management arrangements and contracts are clearer, then there is a reduced likelihood of misunderstanding, and the parties can concentrate on the substance of the work. Sharing a clear understanding of what needs to be done will always help.

In future, client organisations in the non-profit sector are likely to place greater emphasis on risk management, and this could affect their dealings with consultants. It may become the norm for individual freelance consultants to be required to hold professional indemnity insurance and to prove the adequacy of their insurances, a practice that is already a standard requirement for most major donors. Client organisations may seek to avoid legal and insurance liabilities by asking consultants to sign contracts that release the client from responsibilities for the health and safety of the consultants. Contracts could require consultants to testify that they have taken reasonable health precautions, and will avoid taking risks or absolve the client of responsibility for certain problems that may occur. This would be a reasonable reaction if client agencies increasingly feared being sued by consultants for negligence.

Of course, wherever possible, the parties involved should look for ways of resolving disagreements through arbitration, rather than resorting to legal action.

Finally

In this book we have suggested that some modest changes should help to make consultancy exercises more effective and more satisfying for all involved. As consultancies improve, it will become easier to promote approaches that allow for better reflection and learning for all.

Annex 1: | Sample contract clauses

This annex provides examples of clauses that are commonly used in consultancy contracts. They can be adapted to meet the needs of particular clients. Note that the examples, taken from various sources, include a mixture of formulations and phrases (for example, *agreement, contract, assignment*); within any specific contract the terminology should be consistent. Some clauses refer to *the Consultant*, and some use *You*: again, consistency is important.

Definitions and description

- State the title of the consultancy.
- Briefly describe the work and refer to the Terms of Reference.
- Define the different parties to the contract, so that the generic terms *client* and *consultant* can be used in other clauses later in the contract.

Title: Consultancy: (evaluation of programme/training/facilitation of a day of reflection, etc.)

Agreement between [the Client, name and address] and [the Consultant, name and address]

Payments

- **Fees:** specify the sums of money to be paid, and the daily rate if applicable.

[Client] will pay the Consultant a fee of [sum of money] per contracted day for the satisfactory completion of the services to be provided, as in the Terms of Reference. The total number of days to be paid will not exceed [number]. No other fee payments will be made without the prior written agreement of the Client.

- **Payment schedule:** specify the dates when different sums may be paid.

  The assignment is expected to start on [date] and end on [date]. [Client] agrees to pay a total fee of [sum of money].

  Payment for the assignment will be made in two instalments, half in advance and half on satisfactory completion of the assignment.

- **Reimbursable expenses:** state what is covered, and how claims should be made.

  General overheads: It is agreed that the consultancy fee includes a sum to cover general overheads that would naturally occur in running a consultancy business, such as telephone calls, printing, photocopying, stationery. If you envisage other expenses, please ask [consultancy manager] to authorise these in advance. Any expenses must be supported by receipts.

  Travel expenses and accommodation: Air tickets will be provided by [client].

  Home to airport travel: [Client] will pay reasonable travel expenses up to [sum of money] for each return journey.

  Travel in country: travel and transport in [country] is to be covered in the per diem payment.

  Per diem: for days spent in [city, country], the Consultant will be paid a flat rate of [sum of money] per day. The per diem is deemed to cover all meals and miscellaneous expenses, including local travel.

  No other payments will be made without the prior written agreement of [Client].

- **Currency and method of payment:** state whether payments will be made by cash, cheque, or bank transfer, in which case the following clause could apply:

  Payment will be made in [currency] directly into a bank account specified by you on your invoice. [Client] will pay the bank charges levied by our bank, and you will pay charges levied by your own bank.

- **Presentation of invoices:** give details of how to submit invoices; plus any other documentation required for audit purposes – timesheets, receipts, and ticket stubs, etc.

An invoice for fees and expenses should be submitted after [specified input] and again after [second specified input or deliverable].

The Consultant must attach to the invoice a signed timesheet, and original receipts for all items claimed.

Claims not properly receipted cannot normally be reimbursed.

All invoices should be submitted to [staff member of client organisation].

[Client] will settle invoices on satisfactory completion of the work.

If the client is contracted by another contractor to do the work, the clause may read:

[Client] will settle invoices on satisfactory completion of the work in terms of acceptance by the Contractor for the report or other output/s for which the Consultant is responsible, as given in the Consultant's Terms of Reference. Payment will normally be made within 30 days of receipt of invoice.

Or

[Client] will endeavour to make payment within 30 days, but reserves the right to withhold payment pending receipt of the corresponding sum from the Contractor.

Conditions for starting and stopping work

Dates may already have been specified in the clauses concerning definitions or payment details, but they could be stated as part of a set of clauses on starting and stopping the work.

- **Start date** of the contract (note that the start date of operational work may be different).
- **End date**(s) for the work and for the contract.
- How **alterations or modifications** can be made.

  No variation to this Agreement shall be valid unless recorded in writing and signed by both parties.

  Or:

  This Agreement may not be altered, changed, supplemented, or amended, except in writing and signed by an authorised representative of each party.

- **Termination of the contract by the client:** the client usually has the right to terminate a contract without giving a reason, but must provide notice in writing to the consultant. The client may be obliged to pay a certain proportion of the fees if it is decided to end the contract in this way. There is usually a clause that applies to both parties to cover premature termination.

  Either party may terminate this agreement by giving one month's written notice to the other party. No compensation is payable on termination of this agreement for any cause.

- **Force majeure:** if the donor withdraws from the project, or *force majeure** applies:

  The Client may terminate this Agreement with immediate effect by giving written notice to the Consultant if the donor contract is terminated at any time for any reason including the reasons given in the donor contract itself including grounds of force majeure.

  *Force majeure would be defined elsewhere in the contract; it covers events beyond the control of either the Client or the Consultant; for example, natural disasters, insecurity, or war, which would make it impossible or unreasonable to carry out the work specified in the contract. It is necessary to describe the procedure by which the contract can be brought to an end.

  In the event of the Agreement being terminated, the Consultant shall take such steps as are necessary to bring the work to an end in a cost-effective, timely, and orderly manner. The Consultant shall submit an account in writing which shall state the amount claimed, taking into account all fees and costs properly incurred or committed by the Consultant in relation to this Agreement or its termination and which cannot be recovered.

  The Client will pay all fees, expenses and other sums due and outstanding under the terms of agreement up to and including the date of termination.

  The Client will reimburse all reasonable expenses necessarily incurred by the consultant after the date of termination in winding up this Agreement.

  And in case the consultant fails to do the work or behaves badly:

  We reserve the right to terminate the contract without notice if you commit a serious breach of this agreement.

Or:

This Agreement may be terminated by the Client by notice in writing before the end of the term in the event that the Consultant is in default under this Agreement or his/her employees or agents act in a way which is prejudicial to the good reputation of the Client. In the event, payments due to the Consultant shall be made for fees and expenses properly incurred up to the date of termination, less any outstanding balance of any advance made. No other payments shall be made.

- **Termination of the contract by the consultant:** the consultant must be able to end a contract if the client behaves badly or makes it impossible or unreasonably difficult for the consultant to carry out the work in the contract. The consultant would normally be allowed to end the contract if he or she had not been paid despite submitting invoices correctly, or if the work were delayed beyond a reasonable length of time.

- **Management of disputes:**

  Both parties agree to endeavour to settle amicably any dispute arising from the execution or interpretation of this Agreement. In the absence of an amicable settlement, any dispute or difference arising out of or in connection with this Agreement shall be determined under English Law.

- **The legal system under which conflict would be resolved:**

  This Agreement shall be governed by and in accordance with the laws of England and Wales, and shall be subject to the non-exclusive jurisdiction of the English courts.

The general sections of a contract may contain the following sections.

Duties of the consultant

- **Standards of behaviour and discipline:** consultants agree to do their best, to inform the client of difficulties, to deliver original material, to avoid defaming the client in any way, etc.

  You will ensure that the services are performed with reasonable care and skill, and according to professional standards which could reasonably be expected from a properly qualified and experienced consultant.

  Or:

  The Consultant agrees to perform the work set out in the Terms of Reference using his/her best endeavours and in accordance with the time schedule provided by the Client:

To inform the Client immediately of any events which may affect the Consultant's ability to perform his/her designated tasks,

To provide reports based on original work and not to infringe the intellectual property of a third party to the Agreement,

To warrant that all work submitted as part of this consultancy is original, is not defamatory, does not infringe the right of any third party, and is not in any way unlawful.

- **Conflict of interest:** the consultant affirms that he or she is free to work on the contract and has no interests or commitments that would prevent the work being performed with integrity and professional detachment. The contract may include statements that the consultant is not currently employed by another part of the client organisation, or has not done so much work for the client organisation as to risk being seen to lack objectivity.

- **Confidentiality:** several clauses prohibiting use of information obtained during the consultancy are usually included:

Confidential information

All information relating to [client organisation's] business, affairs, products, trade secrets, expertise, personnel, customers and suppliers which may reasonably be regarded as confidential information shall hereinafter be referred to as 'confidential information'. You undertake not to disclose, either directly or indirectly, any confidential information that you may acquire in any manner and you further undertake to use all confidential information disclosed to you exclusively for the provision of this Agreement.

Exceptions to confidentiality

The provisions of this clause shall not apply to you in respect of any information if you can prove, by documentary evidence produced to [client organisation] within 28 days of disclosure, that such confidential information

was already in your possession before the disclosure to you under this Agreement
is at the time of disclosure to you available or subsequently becomes available to the public otherwise than through any act or default of yours
is disclosed to you as a matter of right by a third party
is developed by you with dependence directly or indirectly upon disclosure of confidential information by [client organisation]

is disclosed by third parties as a result of unexpected actions beyond your knowledge and/or control.

- **Subcontracting:** the conditions (if any) under which the consultant may pass part of the work to other people.

  The Consultant agrees not to assign any part of his/her duties or work covered by this contract without the Client's written consent.

  Or:

  Except with the prior written consent of [client organisation] you may not assign or sub-contract your rights or obligations under this Agreement.

- **Reporting:** the nature of the report is usually covered in detail in the Terms of Reference and is usually referred to in the contract only as one of the deliverable products of the contract, or as a condition for release of payment.

- **Tax responsibilities:** under English law, particular phrases are used to make it clear that the consultant is responsible for his or her own tax:

  The Consultant will at all times be responsible for his/her own tax and national insurance contributions or local taxes. An employee–employer relationship between the Consultant and the Client will not arise.

  Or:

  Under this contract for services you will be treated as self-employed and therefore liability for paying income tax and national insurance contributions will rest with you, and [client organisation] will make no deduction for these liabilities.

  This agreement constitutes a contract for services to which the provisions of the Employment Rights Act 1996 do not apply.

  At no time during the period covered by the Agreement will a contract of employment exist between yourself and [client organisation].

- **Insurance and liabilities:**
  If the consultant is entirely responsible for his or her own insurance:

  The Consultant is responsible for ensuring adequate and appropriate medical insurance cover before beginning work overseas under a [client organisation] contract for services. The Consultant's fee, as indicated in [clause, paragraph, section] of the contract, is deemed to include an element to cover the cost of medical insurance.

If the client agrees to cover the consultant for certain risks and includes the consultant in the company policy:

You will be covered by [Client] company insurance policy while on official duty [perhaps with some qualification of residence]. Note that the policy contains a condition that 'the insured person must exercise reasonable care to prevent illness, accident, loss or damage'. Underwriters expect proper vaccinations and malarial prophylactics etc. be taken under this condition. Failure to do so prejudices any rights under the policy.

- **Use of the client's name and contact with the media:**

You may not use [Client]'s name for any purpose beyond the performance of your obligations to [Client] unless you have first obtained consent in writing.

- **Use and care of equipment provided by the client:**

The Consultant shall use all reasonable endeavours to ensure that equipment is used in a proper and workmanlike manner and at the conclusion of this Agreement shall apply for instructions from the Client for the disposal of the equipment and shall arrange to dispose of the equipment in accordance with such instructions.

- **Follow-on work:** if the consultant is offered more work as a result of this contract, he or she agrees to refer it to the client.

The Consultant agrees that any follow-on work which is a direct result of this assignment, or through contacts made in the course of this assignment which occurs within six months of the end date of this contract would be contracted through [client organisation].

Duties of the client

- **Confidentiality:** a parallel clause echoing the duties of the consultant may be included; but it is more common to find the duties of both parties made clear in a single set of clauses:

In respect of all information communicated to it on a confidential basis in connection with the Assignment, each party undertakes to treat such information as confidential.

A clause directed only at the Client:

Client agrees to treat as confidential, not only during the term of this Agreement but for three years after the end date of this contract, any manufacturing or trade secrets or business confidence communicated to it by the Consultant in relation to work performed under this Agreement, over and above the mere skill of the Company's profession, the disclosure of which might prejudicially affect the business of the Consultant or of the Consultant's clients.

Such a clause would be followed by exemptions similar to those applying to the Consultant's responsibilities. These would exclude information that would not be considered confidential because it was already in the public domain, or was already known to the client, or developed by the client, or obtained by right, or required to be disclosed by law. Such a provision is clearly limited to information of commercial value to the consultant.

- **Facilities:** state what facilities and services are provided for the use of the consultant.
- **Support:** state what support the client will provide in terms of getting permits or visas and providing introductions, etc.
- **Data protection:** define how the client may use information relating to the consultant.

Annex 2: | Example of a letter of agreement

The following text is based on an actual letter of agreement used as a contract for a consultancy. The client was sub-contracted by another client (Client 2), who had a contract for the work from the European Union. In a direct contract, the fourth paragraph would simply refer to the client's own system of reimbursing costs incurred.

LETTER OF AGREEMENT

Address
Date

Dear

On behalf of [Client] I am pleased to confirm that we accept your offer to carry out this assignment in accordance with the attached Terms of Reference.

The assignment commenced on [date] and will end on [date] and is expected to take a total of [number] days during this period.

[Client] agrees a total fee of [sum of money] representing [number] days at a daily rate of [sum of money].

You may invoice us separately for travel expenses and daily subsistence in accordance with the European Union's norms and the attached contract with Client 2. Payment will be made by [Client] upon receipt of your claim and reimbursement to [Client] by [Client 2].

Three payments will be made upon satisfactory completion of the phases of work outlined in the attached Terms of Reference, and upon receipt of your invoices.

As you are self-employed, responsibility for paying income tax and national insurance will rest with you, and [Client] will make no deductions for these liabilities.

All information arising from the assignment is confidential to [Client], and any reports produced remain the sole property of [Client].

The agreement constitutes a contract for services to which the provisions of the Employment Protection (Consolidation) Act 1978 do not apply. At no time will a contract of employment exist between yourself and [Client].

With best wishes for a successful assignment.

Annex 3: | Cancellation fees

The uncertain nature of work in international consultancy makes it likely that from time to time work will be cancelled. If this happens at short notice, it can mean loss of income for a consultant, and it may be appropriate to request cancellation fees. A consultant would have to judge whether or not to pursue payment of cancellation fees if the client was reluctant to pay.

It could be helpful for a consultant to give a client his or her rates for cancellations when first making contact, so that the matter can be discussed before any difficulties arise. Relatively few of the consultants in our survey had a scheme for cancellation fees.

Box A1: Sample cancellation fees

CONSULTANCY [name]

Following receipt of a signed work contract, and/or confirmation of work by e-mail, the following cancellation fees are applicable:

15+ days' notice: 33% of fee

8–14 days' notice: 50% of fee

1–7 days' notice: 95% of fee

No notice: 100% of fee

Any agreed expenses incurred prior to the start date of the work will be reimbursed upon receipt of appropriate documentation.

We are grateful to Sue Enfield for this example of cancellation fees.

Some observers found these rates rather high and suggested instead something more generous to the client. For example:

15+ days' notice:	25% of fee
8–14 days' notice:	50% of fee
1–7 days' notice:	75% of fee
No notice:	90% of fee

Annex 4 | Consultancy contract or staff contract?

Table A1 is based on a checklist developed by Oxfam GB to help staff to identify the type of work that needed to be done and therefore the type of contract that should be used. It lists many of the essential differences between a consultancy and a temporary staff appointment.

Table A1: Checklist to distinguish a contract for services (a consultancy agreement) from a contract of service (an employment contract)		
Key criteria	Consultant (contract FOR services)	Employee (contract OF services)
Place of work	Not normally on the client company's premises	On the premises of the employing company
Payment	Fees for services are paid against an invoice. Responsibility for national insurance and tax are borne by the individual.	Payment is made through employer's payroll department. The employing company is responsible for deducting national insurance and tax payments.
Provision of employment benefits: sick pay, pension contributions, holiday pay, etc.	The client company provides no employment benefits.	Standard benefits are provided by the employing company.
Expenses	The individual can claim assignment-related expenses as specified in the contract.	All support and material are provided by the employing company.

Insurance (loss or damage to equipment, public liability, etc.)	The individual is responsible for obtaining personal cover covered by the client company's policies.	The individual is covered by the employing company's policies.
Equipment and administrative support	Equipment and admin support are normally supplied by the individual consultant.	Equipment and admin support are supplied by the employing company.
Nature and degree of supervision	The individual is not supervised by staff of the client company as part of line management. He or she will generally report to a designated contract manager.	The individual is supervised by staff of the employing company.
Frequency of work	Irregular assignments	Consecutive regular assignments
Independence	The individual is free to work for others.	The employing company controls and supervises the hours worked.
Termination of contract	The contract ends when the job is complete (with no notice period).	The contract ends with a period of notice.

Annex 5 | Sample contents of a Call for Tenders

This annex is designed to advise those who are drawing up an invitation to tender for a consultancy assignment. As it shows what the person managing the tender process will be expecting, it may also be helpful to consultants who are drawing up a tender.

Introduction
- Explain who is eligible to tender. (Individuals or organisations from within a specific geographical area?)
- Emphasise the importance of following the format given.
- State that the client is not bound to accept the lowest tender or any tender, and that the client reserves the right to request any or all of the tenderers to attend a meeting to clarify their proposals.

Format
- Specify the language in which the tender should be written, the size and type of paper, the style of binding, etc.
- Specify the required table of contents: summary, technical contents, timetable, financial information, and budget.

Technical contents
- State whether you expect tenderers to comment on the Terms of Reference (and if so, the level of detail that you expect). (This depends on how much scope you have for modifications to the ToR at a later stage.)

- Specify the level of detail required in the tenderer's description of the approach and methods that will be used.
- Specify the format for names and CVs of personnel.
- Ask for a breakdown of the days and timing of the inputs of the various members of the team, perhaps in the form of a Gantt chart or similar.

Financial matters

- Ask the tenderer to confirm acceptance of the terms of your proposed contract.
- Ask for a very clear breakdown of fees and expenses to be charged.
- Ask for a clear listing of names and roles of selected personnel.

Financial information could be set out in tables like these:

1. Costs of personnel

Name	Country	No. of days	Daily rate	Cost

2. Expenses

	Details and rates	Cost
Travel		
Daily living costs		
Equipment		
Other		
Total		

3. Timetable /schedule of payments

Criteria for payment might be completion and acceptance of specified parts of the work, including provision of a deliverable product such as a written report.

Criteria for payment	Amounts to be paid
Total	

Personnel

- Ask for confirmation that all team members will be available to provide the services required of them for the duration of the project. State whether or not you require Confirmation of Availability forms for each member of the team (see the end of this annex for sample forms).
- (If appropriate) ask for confirmation that all team members have the necessary permission from employers or previous employers to participate in the project.

Alternative tenders

It may be useful to allow tenderers to propose other ways of getting the work done, in an alternative tender which would accompany a conventional response to the Invitation to Tender.

- (If appropriate) invite tenderers to submit an alternative tender as a separate offer, clearly marked and accompanying the primary tender.
- The alternative tender must include all necessary technical and financial details, to enable consideration alongside other tenders.

Tax

Emphasise that tenderers are responsible for identifying all applicable tax liabilities and are expected to show this information in the financial section of the tender.

Alterations

Specify that all alterations must be made in writing and signed by the person submitting the tender.

Declarations

Ask tenderers to provide Declarations covering the following issues to accompany their tenders.

- That the tenderer has examined the information provided in your Invitation to Tender and that they offer to undertake the work described in accordance with requirements as set out in the Invitation. The tender should specify the duration of its validity, on the understanding that you may accept it at any time before that expiry date.
- That the tenderer understands that the tender, if accepted, will form part of the contract that will be issued.

- That the tender has been developed independently and without consulting or entering into any kind of agreement with any other group who are tendering for the contract.
- That the tenderer agrees to bear the costs of preparation and submission of the tender and to bear any further pre-contract costs.

If the tender is a joint venture with another agency, the tenderer should provide a copy of the agreement between their organisations.

The tender should be signed by an individual who can confirm that he or she has the authority of their organisation to submit tenders and to clarify any details on its behalf.

Presentation and delivery of tenders

- Tenders must be delivered in sealed envelopes clearly labelled with the contract title, reference number, due date, and tenderer's name.
- Tenders must be received at [address] by [time] on [date].
- Late tenders will not be accepted in any circumstances and will be returned unopened.

Disclosures

- Tenderers must disclose details of any circumstances, including personal, financial, and business activities, that will or might give rise to a conflict of interest. Tenderers should explain how they will avoid any potential conflicts of interest that they identify. [Client] reserves the right to reject any tender which in [client]'s opinion gives rise to, or could potentially give rise to, a conflict of interest.
- Any criminal convictions or criminal proceedings.

Client's obligations

Provide a list of your own obligations:

- To ensure that tenders are registered and held securely.
- To ensure that tenders are opened before witnesses.
- To ensure that all tenders are evaluated objectively in accordance with the criteria contained in the Invitation to Tender.
- To inform tenderers within [number of days] of the decisions made.
- To provide feedback to tenderers within [number of days] if requests for feedback are received in writing.

Sample statements of availability

Each CV submitted for each member of the proposed team could be accompanied by a signed statement of availability.

- [Project name/Contract number] I, the undersigned, agree to participate with the Tenderer [name] in the above-mentioned service-tender procedure. I declare that, in the event that the tender is successful, I am able and willing to work for the period(s) foreseen, in the role for which my CV has been included.
- By making this declaration, I understand that if I fail to certify the above I will be excluded from this tender procedure.

A statement of exclusive availability to one tenderer

Name of agency and all members of the joint venture (if appropriate):
....

Contract: [name and number]: ....

I confirm that I have agreed to be nominated by the above-named consortium of companies for this proposal. I also confirm my availability for the project and my exclusivity to this consortium.

Signature: ....

Date: ....

A statement of non-exclusive availability

I confirm that I have agreed to be nominated by the above-named consortium of companies for this proposal. I also confirm my availability for the project.

Conflict of interest

I confirm that I have no conflict of interest and no concurrent assignments with [client], and no work history with more than 15 per cent working days with [client].

Annex 6 | Fee-calculation tables

This annex illustrates several ways of calculating fee rates.

Table A2: Annual gross income, calculated on the basis of the average daily rate earned and the number of paid days							
	Number of paid days						
Average daily rate	80	100	120	140	160	180	200
100	8000	10000	12000	14000	16000	18000	20000
120	9600	12000	14400	16800	19200	21600	24000
140	11200	14000	16800	19600	22400	25200	28000
160	12800	16000	19200	22400	25600	28800	32000
180	14400	18000	21600	25200	28800	32400	36000
200	16000	20000	24000	28000	32000	36000	40000
220	17600	22000	26400	30800	35200	39600	44000
240	19200	24000	28800	33600	38400	43200	48000
260	20800	26000	31200	36400	41600	46800	52000
280	22400	28000	33600	39200	44800	50400	56000
300	24000	30000	36000	42000	48000	54000	60000
320	25600	32000	38400	44800	51200	57600	64000
340	27200	34000	40800	47600	54400	61200	68000
360	28800	36000	43200	50400	57600	64800	72000
380	30400	38000	45600	53200	60800	68400	76000
400	32000	40000	48000	56000	64000	72000	80000
420	33600	42000	50400	58800	67200	75600	84000
440	35200	44000	52800	61600	70400	79200	88000
460	36800	46000	55200	64400	73600	82800	92000
480	38400	48000	57600	67200	76800	86400	96000
500	40000	50000	60000	70000	80000	90000	100000
520	41600	52000	62400	72800	83200	93600	104000
540	43200	54000	64800	75600	86400	97200	108000
560	44800	56000	67200	78400	89600	100800	112000
580	46400	58000	69600	81200	92800	104400	116000
600	48000	60000	72000	84000	96000	108000	120000

For example; if a consultant were able to obtain an average daily rate of 360, he or she would have to work 100 paid days in order to obtain a gross annual income of 36,000. However, if he or she could average only 300 per paid day, it would be necessary to work 120 paid days in order to earn 36,000.

Table A3: Average daily rate, calculated on the basis of required annual gross income and number of paid days

Annual gross income	Number of paid days												
	80	90	100	110	120	130	140	150	160	170	180	190	200
20000	250	222	200	182	167	154	143	133	125	118	111	105	100
30000	375	333	300	273	250	231	214	200	188	176	167	158	150
40000	500	444	400	364	333	308	286	267	250	235	222	211	200
50000	625	556	500	455	417	385	357	333	313	294	278	263	250
60000	750	667	600	545	500	462	429	400	375	353	333	316	300
70000	875	778	700	636	583	538	500	467	438	412	389	368	350
80000	1000	889	800	727	667	615	571	533	500	471	444	421	400
90000	1125	1000	900	818	750	692	643	600	563	529	500	474	450
100000	1250	1111	1000	909	833	769	714	667	625	588	556	526	500

If a consultant requires a gross annual income of 40,000 and wants to work only 80 paid days in a year, he or she will have to charge an average daily rate of 500. If he or she is able to work 130 paid days in a year, it will be possible to charge an average daily rate of 308.

Table A4: Number of paid days, calculated on the basis of the average daily rate and required annual gross income

	Average daily rate											
Annual gross income	100	150	200	250	300	350	400	450	500	550	600	Annual gross income
20000	200	133	100	80	67	57	50	44	40	36	33	20000
30000		200	150	120	100	86	75	67	60	55	50	30000
40000			200	160	133	114	100	89	80	73	67	40000
50000				200	167	143	125	111	100	91	83	50000
60000					200	171	150	133	120	109	100	60000
70000						200	175	156	140	127	117	70000
80000							200	178	160	145	133	80000
90000								200	180	164	150	90000
100000									200	182	167	100000

(We have not included calculations for 200+ days, since we think it unlikely that a consultant could work more than 200 paid days in any one year.)

Notes

1 'Guide to Buying and Managing Consultants and Providers of Professional Services', by Christopher Bouverie-Brine and Peter Parry (Sterling Management Consultants, 2000) prepared for the training of Oxfam GB staff. In its turn, this material draws on a publication by the same authors: *Professional Advice and Services: A Good Practice Guide* (The Stationery Office, 1999).

2 M. Kubr (1997) *How to Select and Use Consultants. A Client's Guide*, Management Development Series No 31, Geneva: International Labour Office, second edition.

3 Kubr, *op.cit.*, p.17.

4 www.act-assn.dircon.co.uk.

5 *Process Consultation: Lessons for Managers and Consultants*, Addison-Wesley, 1987.

6 IFRC (2002) *Handbook for Monitoring and Evaluation*, Geneva: IFRC (International Federation of Red Cross and Red Crescent Societies).

7 *Flawless Consulting: A Guide to Getting Your Expertise Used*, second edition, Pfeiffer, 1999.

8 IFRC, *op. cit.*

9 Kubr, *op.cit.*, p. 80

10 Some samples relevant to consultants and trainers appear on the website of the British Quality Foundation: www.quality-foundation.co.uk/cgi-bin/ pi_consultantsregister.cgi?page=0402).

11 www.mdn.org.uk

12 Sterling Management Consultants, 2000. See note (1).

13 Based on Sterling Management Consultants, 2000. See note (1).

14 These clauses are reproduced with permission from contracts issued by Oxfam GB and Information Training and Development (ITAD Ltd.), a consultancy company based in Hove, UK (www.itad.com).

15 Based on Sterling Management Consultants, 2000. See note (1).

16 IFRC, *op.cit.*

Annotated bibliography

Books on consulting and consultation

Arthur, L., and R. Preston, with C. Ngahu, S. Le Breton, and D. Theobold (1996) *Quality in Overseas Consultancy: Understanding the Issues*, London: The British Council
This is the only text that we have found which deals with consulting in international development. It contains a great deal of excellent material, but the small typeface makes it difficult to read. Can be obtained free, but only directly from the British Council in the UK (telephone 44 (0)161 957 7755).

Bacal, Robert (2002) *The Complete Idiot's Guide to Consulting*, Indianapolis: Alpha
This book is mainly for consultants working in the commercial sector, but it has a good chapter on ethics in consulting.

Bellman, Geoffrey M. (2002) *The Consultant's Calling: Bringing who you are to what you do*, Jossey-Bass, second edition
An excellent book about what it means to be a consultant. Easy to read. Recommended to consultants who feel that too much of their life is given to work.

Block, P. (1981/2000) *Flawless Consulting: A Guide to Getting your Expertise Used*, Jossey-Bass/Pfeiffer
A serious book about being a consultant. Contains some very useful observations and exercises, but it should be noted that the focus is on commercial consultations in the USA.

Cope, Mick (2003) *The Seven Cs of Consulting: The Definitive Guide to the Consulting Process*, Prentice Hall
One of the many texts about working as a management consultant. It deals very well with conditions that make it more likely that the client will make changes as a result of a consultancy input.

Kara, H. and P. Muir (2003) *Commissioning Consultancy: Managing Outside Expertise to Improve your Services*, Russell House Publishing
An excellent book and one of the very few that is not focused on management consulting in the private sector. An easy style but with some specifically British phrases.

Kubr, Milan (ed.) (1976/2002) *Management Consulting: A Guide to the Profession*, Geneva: International Labour Office
Probably one of the most influential texts on consulting. A huge book, which can only be used as a reference. As you read other texts, you will recognise bits of this one.

Kubr, Milan (1993/1997) *How to Select and Use Consultants. A Client's Guide*, Management Development Series No 31, Geneva: International Labour Office
A much more usable book than Kubr's earlier giant work. Consultants can make good use of this book, even though it is addressed to clients. It includes clear statements on how consultants can help and how they are used, and good sections on how consultants calculate their fees, and on the importance of evaluating consultancies.

Schein, Edgar H. (1987) *Process Consultation*, Addison Wesley OD Series, Volume II
A highly influential writer on consultation, presenting some interesting ideas. Narrowly focused on management consultancies in the private sector. Some nice stories to illustrate that even famous and successful consultants find some jobs very difficult!

Sterling Management Consultants (1999) *Professional Advice and Services: A Good Practice Guide*, prepared for the Further Education Funding Council and National Audit Office and published by The Stationery Office, London
A simple presentation of steps involved in recruiting and making the best use of consultants. Very focused on the UK education sector, but contains some observations that apply to all consultancies. Based on lists, some of which are very long. Contains a strong endorsement of the need to evaluate consultancies.

Books about monitoring and assessing international development

Chambers, Robert (2005) *Ideas for Development,* London: Earthscan
An excellent review of evolving ideas in international development over the last thirty years, written in a very readable style. We specifically recommend the section concerned with the various meanings attributed to the word 'participation'.

Gosling, L. with M. Edwards (1995) *Toolkits: A Practical Guide to Assessment, Monitoring, Review and Evaluation,* London: Save the Children UK
Still a sound text, covering all the key aspects of international development projects.

IFRC (2002) *Handbook for Monitoring and Evaluation,* Geneva: International Federation of Red Cross and Red Crescent Societies
A good text on evaluations. Although it is addressed to people who manage evaluations, it describes some of the difficulties that consultants face when trying to evaluate projects in international development.

Other books

Handy, Charles (1991) *The Age of Unreason,* London: Century Business
A major writer on how organisations work, and how people cope with change.

Index

Page references for material in figures, tables, or boxes are in italic
'An' indicates material in the Annexes